"They Treated Us
Just Like Indians"

Studies in the Anthropology of
North American Indians

EDITORS
Raymond J. DeMallie
Douglas R. Parks

"They Treated Us Just Like Indians"

The Worlds of Bennett County, South Dakota

PAULA L. WAGONER

Published by the
University of Nebraska Press
Lincoln and London

In cooperation with the
American Indian Studies
Research Institute,
Indiana University,
Bloomington

All photographs courtesy of the author.
Portions of this work appeared elsewhere in earlier form and are reprinted
with permission: Paula L. Wagoner
(1997b) Surveying Justice: The
Problematics of Overlapping Jurisdictional Domains in Indian Country.
Droit et cultures 33 (1) 21–52; Wagoner (1998a) Coming Home to What?
The Poetics of Non-Meaning in Martin, South Dakota. *In* Interpreting Cul-
tures: A Symposium, edited by Paula L.
Wagoner and Mindy J. Morgan, 1–7.
Bloomington: Indian University De-
partment of Anthropology; Wagoner
(1998b) An Unsettled Frontier: Land,
Blood, and U.S. Federal Policy. *In*
Property Relations, edited by C. M.
Hann, 124–41. London: Cambridge Uni-
versity Press. Reprinted with the per-
mission of Cambridge University Press.
Library of Congress Cataloging-in-
Publication Data
Wagoner, Paula L. "They treated us
just like Indians": the worlds of
Bennett County, South Dakota / Paula
L. Wagoner, p. cm. – (Studies in
the anthropology of North American
Indians) Includes bibliographical
references and index.
ISBN 0-8032-4800-8 (cloth : alk. paper) –
ISBN 0-8032-9830-7 (pbk. : alk. paper)
1. Teton Indians – South Dakota –
Bennett County. 2. Bennett County
(S.D.) – Race relations. 3. Bennett
County (S.D.) – Social conditions.
4. Teton Indians – Legal status, laws, etc.
5. Pine Ridge Indian Reservation (S.D.)
I. Title. II. Series.
E99.T34 W34 2002 978.3'65 – dc21
2002017963

"𝒩"

Dedicated
respectfully to
those who have
left their mark:

Roy and Lillian Farmer
Bill Tallbull
Grace Whitehorse
Justin McDonald
Jean Smith
Wendell Long
Marge Woods
Vincent and Wilma Richards
Dean Bettelyoun
Ilo Fralick

And to

Sierra and Logan,

who are only
beginning to
make theirs.

CONTENTS

ILLUSTRATIONS

ACKNOWLEDGMENTS

The journey toward this ethnography has been a long one, and there are many people to thank for their good counsel and support. Beginning at the long-postponed undergraduate level is Mercedes Batty, at Sheridan College, and Eleanor Rothman, director of the Ada Comstock Scholars Program at Smith College. Also from my Smith years I especially wish to thank Neal Salisbury for his faith in me, Arturo Escobar, Triloki Madan, Frédérique Marglin, Don Joralemon, Peter d'Errico at the University of Massachussetts, Amherst, and all the others who began the difficult process of challenging my assumptions.

I also wish to express deep gratitude to my mentors and friends from the Indiana University years: Raymond J. DeMallie for always making time for me and quietly breaking trail, leaving subtle guideposts for me to find, and innumerable blessings; Carol Greenhouse – an indefatigable optimist – for providing a model of excellence in mentoring and for keeping a perpetually open office door where many of us felt free enough to cry tears of frustration and of joy; R. David Edmunds for his humor, irreverence, and most un-subtle prodding; Anya Peterson Royce for her delight in mentoring women through the process and the intuition that led her to know when a hug was needed; Vine Deloria, Jr., for that serendipitous meeting at Harvard, the cup of coffee at Geo's on Main Street in Martin, South Dakota, and the late-night e-mail; Bonnie Kendall for teaching me to teach and reminding me that under-graduates need good mentors too; Paul Jamison for crossing the so-called sociocultural-bioanthropological border to offer criticisms that enabled me to think about my research in different ways; and Connie Adams, Debra Wilker-son, and Rita Crouch for their cheerful handling of often hysterical phone calls from the field.

The people of Bennett County who so generously opened their lives to me deserve special thanks for putting up with my questions and my presence with warmth and dignity. My life has been enhanced immeasurably by knowing them and experiencing firsthand their abundant rural hospitality. I wish to thank a few individuals who were especially kind: Shirley Big Eagle, Pastor Kate Bottorff, Shirley and Bob Claussen, Pearl Cottier, Dorthea DuBray, Roy, Lillian, and David Farmer, Patty Fralick, Tory Hoblit, Ray Howe, Donna Jackson, Emma and Lee Jacobs, Ruth Jaquot, Ardeth Kocourek, Leonard Little Finger, Lawrence Long, Mary and Wendell Long, Art McDonald, Justin McDonald, Donna Mattson, Boyd Richards and Shirley Marshall, Martha and Ron Riggs, Paul Robertson, Father Parke Street, Joyce and Chuck Tutsch, Grace, Louie and Wyatt Whitehorse, Marge Woods, Alice Young, Zane Zieman, and my students and the staff at Oglala Lakota College centers in Kyle and Martin. I am also indebted to unnamed others who spent their valuable time talking to me about Bennett County and Pine Ridge Reservation. I will fondly remember Friday night dinners at Markota with the Oglala Lakota College crew: Greg and Ellen Gagnon, Ursula Gaertner, Jim and Caroline Johnston, Barb and Ray Kerns-Zucco, Devona Lone Wolf, and all the passers-through who donated a semester or two of their time to the college. All persons who granted me formal interviews were given the opportunity to review their statements to amend any "misremembered" information, advise me of clarifications, and offer new perspectives. In each case, I was given permission to include their voices and certain additional, later recollections.

I am deeply indebted to Juniata College and the Department of Sociology, Anthropology, Criminal Justice, and Social Work for allowing me time to finish my dissertation during the first semester of my employment, and for an academic schedule that allows me summers to work on projects such as this one. A special thanks goes to Sarah DeHaas for reading an earlier version of this manuscript and to Bob Reilly for listening to me read portions of this one.

Archival research was made pleasurable by Alan Perry and Rose DeLuca at the Federal Records Center in Kansas City, Missouri; LaVera Rose at the South Dakota State Archives in Pierre; Julie Lakota and Leonard Little Finger at the Oglala Lakota College archives; and the staff at the McKusick Law Library at the University of South Dakota.

It would have been impossible to complete the research that is the foundation of this book without the generous support of the National Science Foundation and its support of the fieldwork leading to my dissertation (Wagoner 1997a), the Philips Fund at the American Philosophical Society, and the Skomp Fund from the Indiana University Department of Anthropology for sustaining my predissertation fieldwork. I would also like to thank the John D. and Catherine T. MacArthur Foundation for allowing me to participate in an interdisciplinary seminar at the Indiana Center on Global Change and World Peace.

From that experience the value of interdisciplinary discussions became abundantly clear and greatly enlarged the scope of my own future work.

Portions of this revised manuscript have appeared elsewhere in different scholarly venues. I wish to thank C. M. Hann for his close reading of material that related to a chapter prepared for his edited volume entitled *Property Relations,* published by Cambridge University Press. Also, the staff at *Droit et cultures* provided useful critiques of chapter 4. Much of the historical research was conducted for a working paper published by the Indiana Center on Global Change and World Peace at Indiana University (Wagoner 1994); I thank the seminar participants, especially John Lovell, Jack Hopkins, Eduardo Brondizo, Miki Pohl, and the Center staff for criticism and suggestions.

Thomas Biolsi, Karen Blu, and Anne Straus were readers of my unrevised manuscript and offered many useful and insightful suggestions for its improvement. I thank them for the effort they put in on my behalf. Of course, the usual disclaimer applies: any blunders that remain are my own.

I extend grateful thanks to Kate Bottorff and Alice, Willie, Kenya, and Dylan for so graciously opening their home in Pendleton, Oregon, to me. It was a pleasure turning my dissertation into a revised manuscript on their sunny porch, and it was a luxury walking Alice the church dog along the banks of the Umatilla River while thinking things through. I also appreciate Kate's insightful jogging of my memory concerning certain details of my stay in Bennett County. She was there, too, during the events that this book describes. I am also grateful to Laura Marcus for providing a home away from home while in Portland. Her perspectives were most helpful.

Janet and Scott Maxwell provided me unconditional love, emotional support, and a room in Sheridan, Wyoming, when needed. They reminded me that for them, Ph.D. meant "Paula holed-up downstairs," and can be relied upon to keep me in my place, as true friends will do. Also thanks to Caitlin Anderson, Carolyn Anderson, Christina Burke, Dennis Christafferson, Gerardo Dirié, Fran Flavin, Raymond Fogelson, Wally Hooper, Frederick Hoxie, Jason Baird Jackson, Karen Kessel, Wyman Kirk, Martha Knack, Carol Kaminsky, Rick Laurent, Margot Liberty, Jack McDermott, Harvey Markowitz, Michael Moore, Mindy Morgan, Cindy Neil, Doug Parks, Dollie Reno, Sarah Sherry, Brother C. M. Simon, S.J., Carmen Tellez, and Barbara Zang for their support and inspiration. And thank you, Traci and Donna Gibboney, for looking out for my cats during the summers so I could make my getaway. To my cats *Chąté Wašté Wį* 'Goodhearted Woman' and Lucy, thanks for delighting me through many long winters and teaching me that Plato was wrong – in the final analysis it really does come down to shadows dancing.

Finally, I wish to thank Jeff and Lawanda Wagoner for putting up with my long absences, long distance calls, and foremost, for my granddaughter Sierra. They settled the question of whether I would have my dissertation completed before I became a grandmother once and for all. They also proved that I would be a grandmother twice before finishing this manuscript; thank you for also blessing the world with my grandson, Logan. My parents, sisters, and brother are now aware of what I have been doing for so long in such out of the way places.

ORTHOGRAPHY

Because many diverse systems have been used to write Lakota, words cited throughout this volume have been systematically retranscribed to conform to the orthography chosen for University of Nebraska Press Publications (see Rood and Taylor 1996). Special symbols are:

ą nasalized *a*

c voiceless alveolar affricate, pronounced as *tch* in English *watch*

ǧ voiced velar frictave, pronounced as *r* in Parisian pronunciation of *Paris*

h indicates aspiration when following a consonant; thus, for example, the sequence *th* in Lakota is pronounced strongly as *t* in English *toe,* and not as *th* in English *thin*

ȟ unvoiced velar fricative, pronounced as *ch* in German *ach*

į nasalized *i*

š voiceless alveolar fricative, pronounced as *sh* in English *ship*

ų nasalized *u*

ž voiced alveolar fricative, pronounced as *s* in English *vision*

' glottal stop, as in English *oh-oh!*

′ accent mark indicating stress

"They Treated Us
Just Like Indians"

ONE

Introducing Bennett County, South Dakota

Where I live was "the Great American Desert," shunned by all but the hardiest explorers. Later, the thinkers in their comfy New England offices decided that "rain follows the plow," and all that was needed to make the desert bloom were a few hardy souls to build claim shanties and plow to the horizon. The New England philosophers had no idea what difficult conditions westerners faced, but the westerners went right on working until they controlled everything but the weather. HASSELSTROM 1991:325

I had not intended to do fieldwork in Bennett County, South Dakota; in fact, I had never even heard of the place before stopping at this wide spot on Highway 18 for a cup of coffee at Geo's on Main Street. I enjoyed listening to local folks talk about the weather and cuss that cold and dreary June of 1993 as a muddy season that seemed to have no end. I heard terms like "gumbo" and "mudded in," and wondered what they meant and why farmers and ranchers were so disgusted. I saw Indians and non-Indians come in, nod at each other in recognition, and sometimes exchange a few words. I saw people in terms of phenotype back then. Not knowing that most people in the area fell into an ambiguous local social category referred to as "mixedblood," I found it easy to identify locals as dark Indians and light whites. Things seemed pretty clear on my first day in town, and I was confident that I had found some variety of parallel societies that interacted at certain places, such as cafes, schools, and grocery stores, and at church. It all seemed pretty cut and dried, and I thought perhaps a simple structural analysis of existing social relations might do the trick.

By the end of the summer of 1997 when my fieldwork came to an end (as if it ever really ends, given the value and strength in precious and permanent ties that have been forged with adoptive and adopted families), I had come to know how incredibly complex relations are here, and on how many levels. My stay in Bennett County coincided with the period when federal, state, and county budgetary concerns threatened to unravel this place once and for all. This was the moment when non-Indian farmers were forced to acknowledge the magnitude of their own dependence on federal crop disaster relief, federal aid to farmers, and price supports. Proud ranchers and farmers, who had become comfortable with criticizing federal annuities, health care, and other treaty benefits for Indians, had to accept their own dependence on federal price supports and farm programs. Local merchants also recognized their dependence on the business generated by the recipients of those federal programs. The fragile artificial economy was finally recognized and now it had to be confronted.

The only logical place to begin describing Bennett County is with the land that supports this unique combination of overlapping cultures and lifestyles. Why would anyone have chosen this place that passersby call "God-forsaken" to huddle together in small houses scattered around without even as much as a row of lilac bushes to break the wind? How did people only two or three generations back presume that this land would grow wheat when they literally had to use pickaxes to "bust" the prairie sod's thick rhizomes, tightly tangled and compacted up to eight inches deep? How was it that neighbors of different races and ethnic backgrounds thought that they could build a community in spite of dissimilar languages, worldviews, and technologies, in a region where cooperation was essential? And finally, how was it that any of these diverse peoples ever thought that they were destined to be masters of the land?

There is something mythical about living in an area of the country expendable enough for Rand McNally to omit from its 1990 travel atlas.[1] Residents prefer to perceive this place in terms relating to "heartland." While many boast of their proximity to the geographical center – the physical heart – of the United States, which lies less than 150 miles northwest of Bennett County as the crow flies, others know that the Black Hills have always been the spiritual center of the world, even before satellite photographs revealed that they formed the unmistakable shape of a human heart. Still, the greatest number of those hastily traveling through to their ultimate destinations closer to the coasts perceive this area as the long and boring part. I formed my own unshakable first impression of South Dakota on a trip some ten years before. This was a place where grasshoppers the size of mice became ugly smears on the van's grill and smacked up against my arm as we sped along the interstate highway linking Wyoming to Chicago. Weird-looking bugs of grand proportion hung out in the rest areas, making short convenience stops less than convenient, or, for that matter, restful.

But then, as Jean Baudrillard (1989) found while retracing Alexis de Tocqueville's search for democracy in America, interstate travel often merely allows a strange postmodern melange to pass for reality. Just north of Martin, South Dakota, on I-90, one can see for oneself that there is a *real* Wall Drug (after passing about 250 signs advertising "Free Water" and "5 cent coffee" I figured that these were just a nasty joke on thirsty motorists) (see Butler 1994:771), and a *real* Corn Palace, and Reptile Gardens, and the home of Fred and Wilma Flintstone. There is a place where some have blasted the heads of four prominent presidents into a beautiful mountainside, and a place where others are in the process of blowing chunks of Crazy Horse mountain away to expose the Oglala Lakota[2] chief on horseback, pointing toward the horizon. His stature was intended to dwarf the faces of the four presidents carved into Mount Rushmore and happens to dominate the town named for George Armstrong Custer, whom he defeated at the Battle of the Little Bighorn in 1876.

It is only when one exits the efficiently designed interstate highways that southwestern South Dakota shows its stuff. The Badlands have been tamed and civilized enough for any weekend tourist, however, and while many of the interesting places are off-limits by federal regulation, photo opportunities are still abundant. At the southern end of the Badlands one enters the Pine Ridge Indian Reservation, its southeastern quarter being the contested space called Bennett County. This "unremarkable" place became the center of my universe during my two-and-a-half-year stay. It is a place small enough for one to see social and cultural processes in their immediacy, yet large enough to reflect a complicated social and cultural diversity.

The land is in charge here. Despite manmade boundaries that arbitrarily divide it, separating neighbor from neighbor, it persists. As a newcomer, I came to this place where it was not difficult to perceive the seamless vastness of space, but I was not the first. One man described it well: "These vast plains, in which the eye finds no object to rest upon, are first seen as a surprise and a pleasure; but their uniformity at length becomes tiresome" (quoted in Webb 1931: 487). Herbert Quick, also an early traveler, painted another powerful image. "In the spring of 1857 they began their last long trek to a *new and different world.* They turned their faces to the west which they had for generations seen at sunset through traceries of the twigs and leafage of the primal forests, and *finally stepped out into the open, where God had cleared the fields,* and stood at last with the forests behind them, gazing with dazzled eyes sheltered under the cupped hands of toil out over a sea of grassy hillocks, while standing in the full light of the sun. *It was the end of Book One of our history*" (quoted in Webb 1931: 486–87, italics in original). I had to develop the South Dakotan's eye before I realized that the openness was seen locally as smaller, bounded – and often contested – parcels of property. After some practice, I learned to discern the fences and trace them all the way to the horizon, the patchwork quilt of crop and grazing land coming sharply into vision, challenging me to see the land as seamless once again.

Once it became clear that there was a familiar order inscribed upon the prairie land in the county, it became possible to orient myself as I drove the back roads. I learned to ride section lines, which are laid out in neat grids running from north to south and east to west. It was impossible to be an inconspicuous observer on dry days when the dust kicked up by my tires hung in the air like an arrow pointing me out. But on sullen gray days after a rain, when I would not slow down and pay proper respect to the gumbo mud, my car would slide towards the ditch.

Many early observers described the prairie as a vast ocean, and one can try to imagine the fenceless wilderness that they encountered. One described it powerfully: "Like an ocean in its vast extent, in its monotony, and in its danger, it is like an ocean in its romance, in its opportunities for heroism, and in the fascination it exerts on all those who come fairly within its influence. The first experience of the plains, like the first sail with a 'cap' full of wind, is apt to be sickening. This once overcome, the nerves stiffen, the senses expand, and man begins to realize the magnificence of being" (Webb 1931:487). Another described the capricious plains, "For a few days the weather had been fine, with cool breezes and broken flying clouds. The shadows of these coursing rapidly over the plain, seemed to put the whole in motion; and we appeared to ourselves as if riding on the unquiet billows of the ocean" (ibid.). Pioneers headed out in "prairie schooners" mindful of the fact that the Great Plains "are like the *ocean*, in more than one particular; but in none more than this: the utter impossibility of producing any just impression of them by description. They inspire feelings so unique, so distinct from anything else, so powerful, yet vague and indefinite, as to defy description, while they invite the attempt" (ibid.:468).

Yet people did come to define the indefinable, and their fence lines indicate that some attempt has been made to separate one thing from another, maybe a cow from the road, a neighbor from a neighbor, a nation from a nation.

Despite the predictable manmade pattern of fences separating sunflowers from wheat, millet from corn, and grazing pasture from hayfield, I was struck by a persistent, if seemingly inappropriate metaphor for the arid plains – a delta, rather than an ocean. Mixing and interpenetration of distinct elements have always been a part of Bennett County. One day, winds that reached eighty miles per hour blew the county's marginal topsoil south toward the sand hills of Nebraska, and, through some indecipherable logic of reciprocity, the next day's wind returned the favor by depositing sand onto cultivated fields. Those were the days when I wished that I was home putting duct tape around the window frames and covering the air conditioner with plastic to stop dust from filtering in. But, as it turned out, I was usually on the road worrying that my car would suck in too much dust and fall dead, asphyxiated. Dust must be tolerated here; it is a fact of life that complaining cannot deter. People laugh about

1. Mid-afternoon dust storm on Main Street

it. For them, it is just another trick of nature that keeps the outsiders out and the insiders feeling like they have survived yet another test. It will become clear in later chapters that that the notion of an interpenetrating and fluid delta area applies to social relations in this region as well.

It is almost impossible to talk about the land in terms other than human. She has her moods, her pests, her life cycle. She is a living thing that, having preceded humans, does not require their definition. Here, the land is never an empty sign, even when not invested with meaning by those who draw sustenance from her. She will take care of herself; she always has. But it is the tendency of cultural groups to define the land, attempt to control her, and invest her with meaning that concerns me here (see Feld and Basso 1996).

Land is a major element of personal and group identity in this part of the country. One's worth is measured by his or her relationship to it. Whether farmer, rancher, merchant, Indian, non-Indian, town dweller, or country person, here one defines oneself and others in terms of physical proximity to or metaphorical distance from it. One man took exception when I referred to him as a rancher and told me in no uncertain terms that he was a *farmer* who cultivates and nourishes the soil. He proudly told me that farmers are perceived to be "scratching in the dirt" by ranchers and Lakotas. He said that compared

2. Sudden summer dust storm obscuring the Martin watertower

to farmers, ranchers who let their cows run are seen as pretty lazy folks, but are thought to make a lot more money, enabling them to acquire more and more land for their herds. They are perceived as more genteel than farmers, with more time to play (see Jorgensen 1984).

The same type of dichotomy can be observed within the Indian community. Indians who live in the city (i.e., in Pine Ridge Village, Martin, or HUD housing in the districts) often are looked upon as "pitiful" and of a lower class than those who live on their own allotments out in the country. The stereotype of "city" Indians holds that they are devoid of traditional culture and open to more choices, by virtue of their living in town among many kinds of people. HUD residence clusters are perceived locally to be slum areas and to have problems with littered homesteads, graffiti, robbery, alcohol, drugs, and concentrated gang activity (many Lakota teens have learned about gangs through videos and rap music and are "wannabe" members of urban gangs such as the Crips, the Bloods, and the War Lords). "City Indians" are the descendants of Lakotas who were not able to hang onto their allotments and have become assimilated into the lifestyle associated with urban poverty.

But the land is above such divisions. People who live here are all connected to her and her moods. In a blizzard, they walk to the same post office for their mail and huddle together as survivors, lingering over a word or two with neighbors who are suddenly co-conspirators, sharing secrets about how they make it through. They laugh. They shake hands. They trudge their separate ways home.

One watershed moment opened my eyes to what it was to be a human being in South Dakota. I know that it must have been a seminal experience because when I related the story, I was told that I "had arrived." One frigid morning I awoke and peered out my window. There was no discernable horizon. Snow and sky were precisely the same hue, glowing white tinged with the subtle yellow haze of backlighting from the sun somewhere far beyond the clouds. I felt as if inside a snow scene in a glass paperweight. My fieldnotes described the scene:

> Land and sky froze into one another and seemed to fold over upon itself, enclosing the town in a subtly glowing and seamless globe. I experienced an awful sense of claustrophobia that seemed unusual and out of place in the vastness of the Plains. Then an intense mixture of solitude and loneliness flooded over me, further heightening the sense of isolation. True solitude is possible here. But also possible is community at its most fundamental level – neighboring and support.

After that, I wondered how life must have been for Lakotas in this area over a century ago, in scattered winter camps, with only small lodge fires for heat and tipis for shelter. Their non-Indian neighbors were not much better off in their sod houses or wood cabins that sheltered parents, grandparents, and children in a space not much larger than that of a small trailer. I wondered how people managed not to kill one another in a panic of cabin fever, and how they managed to set aside enough wood and provisions to see them through the winter. I did not, however, doubt that neighboring was one of the best parts of pioneer life. Lakotas lived in small, extended family groups, or *thiyóšpaye*, but non-Indian newcomers were pretty much isolated in single-family dwellings, rather far from neighbors and kin. But today, television and videotapes are agents of socialization that have cut into the time for active neighboring. People can be alone and isolated without being cut off from "the world." Such technologies are relatively recent arrivals in Bennett County, having appeared in the 1960s in some locales, but they took root so quickly that they seemed to belong – like the invading Canadian thistles that are as lovely to look at as they are destructive to the health and balance of the plains.

I was prepared to find a community that could be easily described in terms of contrasts. I suspected that in a region shared by Lakotas and non-Indians, ranchers, farmers, and merchants, rich and poor, social lines would be highly defined and resilient. And I suspected that those contrasts would be played out primarily in racial terms. I did find that to some degree, but I also discovered that in this region, residents have more in common than they may care to admit. To be sure, the vernacular of race exists in Bennett County and is deeply ingrained, but years of unselfconscious usage has dulled the meaning in everyday interaction. Not so, however, in times of community crisis. In such situations, the terms "Indian," *iyéska* 'mixedblood' (lit., 'interpreter'), and *wašícu* '(culturally or racially) white person', which are bandied about casually in everyday usage, take on more ominous meanings and emerge as conscious markers of social identity.

One thing that draws people together here is a deep and abiding distrust of outsiders, particularly "Easterners who come here and stir up trouble and then leave." On my first visit to the county library, I introduced myself as a researcher from Indiana University with an interest in the social history of Bennett County, federal policies affecting the region, and social relations in the community. One non-Indian woman was not shy about sharing her feelings with this stranger and bitterly complained about "reformers with big ideas," Easterners who come out to teach at Oglala Lakota College. She referred me to Anne Matthews's book concerning the proposal of two educators from Rutgers University to return the Great Plains to its original state, a virtual buffalo pasture, and move people out (Matthews 1992). She was appalled that Matthews, originally from the region, would become a proponent of Frank and Deborah Popper's hypothesis (see Popper 1984), take up the crusade, and "turn her back on her own people." In her book, the South Dakotan author argues that "during the next generation, as a result of the largest, longest-running agricultural and environmental miscalculations in the nation's history, much of the Plains will become almost totally depopulated. The federal government should begin planning to convert vast stretches of the region to a use so old it predates the American presence – a 'Buffalo Common' of native grass and livestock" (Matthews 1992:307).[3]

This proposal, well-reasoned or not, represents a serious threat to local people, particularly to non-Indians. It is perceived as a nullification of several generations of hard work and suffering on this admittedly marginal farmland. Some of the more "traditional" Lakotas understand such proposals as validating the hunting and gathering past that many elders recall hearing about from their own elders. Much anger is directed at people coming from the northeastern portion of the United States because of their perceived dominance in political decisions at the national level. Many local residents believe that they have again been denied a political voice and put in the position of losing the "place wars."

After all, Easterners who "knew best" settled Lakotas on marginal land and expected them to take up the plow and cultivate – or at least attempt to cultivate – buffalo-grass-covered prairie land. Easterners who "knew best" facilitated the overpopulation of the prairies by recruiting hopeful European immigrants and American emigrants from crowded cities. Those same Easterners then watched judgmentally as, one after another, the unprepared newcomers were forced to move back to the cities to reclaim their positions in the landless underclass labor force. Easterners who "knew best" constructed federal policies regarding Indian people, then modified those policies approximately every thirty years, causing Indians and non-Indians alike to feel alienated on their own land amidst fears that someday the land would be adjudicated out from under them. In short order, as I discovered the Easterners' ubiquitous influence in county affairs, I came to understand the countywide disdain for outsiders purporting to be experts. In addition, I sat through many a dinner with Eastern intellectuals who thought that they knew how to remedy local problems but had not listened to local people long enough to learn that, in many instances, Eastern remedies cannot be implemented in a Western rural *Gemeinshaft*.

Clifford Geertz (1983:73–93) reminds us that what we call "common sense" is dependent upon location and situation, and that what is seen as making sense in one context may be irrational in another. Many outsider intellectuals are, indeed, locally viewed as pathetic people – "they cannot see the forest for the trees." One non-Indian oldtimer pointed out a passage in a book and indicated that it well expressed his feelings: "I once knew an educated lady, banded by Phi Beta Kappa, who told me that she had never heard or seen the geese that twice a year proclaim the revolving seasons to her well-insulated roof. Is education possibly a process of trading awareness for things of lesser worth? The goose who trades his is soon a pile of feathers" (Hasselstrom 1991:63). One cannot argue with that logic. Anti-intellectual suspicion is a constant undercurrent in many rural locales, and Bennett County is no different in that regard.

But that is how it is in small rural communities. There is an impulse toward egalitarianism, and taking oneself too seriously is rewarded with an ample measure of teasing – or ignoring – one back to reality. It is best not to attract too much attention to oneself or try too aggressively to change statuses. Everyone in Martin knows you, knows your parents, and knows exactly where you come from – or soon will. And they will never let you forget.

ANTHROPOLOGICAL PERSPECTIVES ON THE COUNTY
I first read Niels Braroe's *Indian and White* (1975) in graduate school. I remember thinking that it was amazing that some outsider could walk into a border town as a stranger and then leave a few months later with an understanding

of social relationships that even many longtime residents had not considered, at least not consciously. After having been in Bennett County for a couple of years, I realized that the disquiet that I felt in reading Braroe's ethnography was simply a foreshadowing of the problematic experience of participating in and observing community life at the same time.

I chose to live in a small local motel, rather than with a family, in order to keep an "objective" distance from members of the community's three social categories. I did not wish to be identified with any one group and I did not want subconsciously to color my observations by "taking sides." For the first six months of my stay I was able to maintain that stance because I was so new and was simply making my first attempts at clumsy introductions. One member of my dissertation committee had told me that I was fooling myself if I expected to be able to remain completely objective in terms of not privileging one group's concerns, but in my usual arrogant style, I assumed that I could do the impossible. While the (im)possibility of anthropological objectivity has been debated for years, I could not quite shake the notion that it was important, and that I could pull it off. Of course, I was unsuccessful.

Because I designed this as a regional study rather than as one limited to either Lakotas or rural non-Indian South Dakotans, I expected that the design itself would protect me from identifying with anything more than a rural regional identity. However, I found that the decision to remain objective was, in some ways, taken out of my hands by certain members of the local population who assumed that I was viewing daily life through their own social categories. When they realized that I did not share some of the more stereotypical assessments of people, they assumed that I was of some unknown order of human being and moved slightly away from me. This occurred more often among non-Indians and mixedbloods of the upper middle class than among any other groups, perhaps because of the fear that I, as an outsider, might upset the locally negotiated status quo. This same phenomenon had occurred in Braroe's community of Short Grass. Assumptions, not necessarily correct, were made about the ethnographer's point of view. Much of this I had attributed to opinions regarding ethnographers and their studies of bounded communities of "others," and I intended to overcome those issues in this research. I was determined that this study would somehow be able to address the "we" who live in a diverse and problematic multilevel melting pot (or, if you prefer, "salad bowl," in today's multicultural parlance), tied to a globalizing economy that is allegedly run by a social construction called "The Market."[4] I was looking for the *E pluribus unum*.

Over the course of my fieldwork, I conducted informal interviews with members of all three of the local social categories in Bennett County, as well as with individuals who had moved away. Longtime residents and their children shared their life histories and fond remembrances with me. I was particularly interested in discovering changes in social relations between people over time. In addition, to observe social interactions, I attended many local public functions and events such as county fairs, powwows, memorial giveaways, rodeos, court proceedings, and various church services. Many of my observations were of women going about their daily lives, and I learned much from conversations with groups of women as they prepared food for special occasions or crafted quilts. Much of the archival research for this study was conducted in federal and state archives as well as at Oglala Lakota College.

From my observations, certain themes arose that resonated with the theoretical perspectives and methods from several specific bodies of anthropological literature, beginning with the early American school of anthropology. At the turn of the twentieth century, Franz Boas argued that each cultural group has a particular history that must be explored, with attention paid to all aspects of culture. His method, which included detailed description and recording of every aspect of culture ranging from the grandest social structure to artistic motifs on the tiniest artifacts, was intended as a means to refute the generalizations of his contemporaries. Some of those generalizations had led to value-laden categorizations of human beings in terms of race. This study follows the Boasian tradition of situating groups in their historical contexts, but generalizes social *processes* on the basis of social fields that are both discrete and interpenetrating, rather than on the basis of bounded groups of people.

Because of my interest in the work of Neils Braroe (1975) and John W. Bennett (1969, and with Seena B. Kohl 1995), whose research focused on the ethnic and racial diversity of the Northern Plains, I chose the unit of analysis of this study to be primarily a regional one. But to get a clearer picture of Bennett County, it was necessary to concentrate on smaller or larger social fields of interaction at different times, much like adjusting the focus when using a camera's telescopic lens.[5] I could get a more complete understanding of Bennett County's regional identity by sometimes sharpening the focus on relational networks in the immediate field of study and at other times drawing back for a better look at the larger context. Regional identities are the products of networks of smaller and larger fields, and each social field must be considered an artificially bounded portion of a continuum (perhaps "welter" is a better word) of relationships. Anthropologists commonly refer to identities becoming "decentered," as if they are always products of unequal power relationships. Undoubtedly, that is often the case. But those identities are, by their very natures, easily decentered because there is really no absolute center in the not necessarily linear continuum – thus, identities are provisional, and are also dependent upon how the researcher's lens is trained (both conceptually and directionally) in space and time.

Consider for a moment the myriad social fields that exist in any region. One may choose, for example, to observe, describe, and analyze such dynamic relational networks in Bennett County as:

inter-/intra-family
inter-/intra-tribal, state, or national
inter-/intra-racial
inter-/intra-social class
East River/West River, South Dakota
western U.S./eastern U.S.
local/global

Occasionally, divisions at the smaller, community levels are brought into a somewhat symbiotic, if tenuous, harmony in larger social, economic, political, and moral contexts. Individual, local, and regional identities are culturally fluid, in constant social flux. Situational identities are expressed in attitudes and behaviors, not only in terms of conscious and active choices (or, if you prefer, "manipulations"), but rather, are also dependent upon the fields that an observer chooses to analyze. Despite certain stereotypes of rural life as simple and idyllic that may be held by cosmopolites who labor in their small gardens for nature's therapeutic value, Bennett County is not an uncomplicated region. From a distance, things appear to be what they are not, although, in some cases, such stereotypes may be mobilized locally for financial or moral benefit to local businesses. People in Bennett County know what they know and have more savvy than most stereotypes imply.

Different conclusions can be drawn about social relationships, depending upon which tiny bit of the continuum of nested social relationships is being observed at any particular time, and easy generalizations are inappropriate. However, other observers of culture and society, including James R. Walker (1980, 1982), Ella C. Deloria (1944), Scudder Mekeel (1932, 1936), Gordon Macgregor (1946), Stephen Feraca and James Howard (1963), Robert Daniels (1970), Murray Wax et al. (1964) (see also Wax et al. 1989), Rosalie Wax (1971), William K. Powers (1977) and Marla N. Powers (1986), Robert Gay (1984, 1985), Paul Robertson (1995), and Mikael Kurkiala (1997) have all lingered primarily on Pine Ridge Reservation, but have also spent time in Bennett County. They have, for the most part, focused their ethnographic inquiries on Lakotas. In many ways, this study validates their assessments of the behaviors that serve, if problematically, to divide local people into certain social categories. Not much has changed in terms of local ideas of what constitutes those longstanding categories called "fullblood," "mixedblood," and "white." Here, I attempt to capture how those attitudes toward those categories came to be by considering the historical events that led to such predictable behaviors when there is nothing predictable in the forms or arenas in which those behaviors and attitudes become manifest. All societies require historical interpretation and reinterpretation in order to remain adaptive, especially in the course of rapid social change at the national and global levels. The people in Bennett County are the products of their complicated histories, as well as actors who use the past to make sense of the present and direct the future in surprising and unpredictable ways.

In that spirit, this research focuses in part on the social category of mixedblood. Seen as marginal by both fullbloods and whites, mixedbloods may take advantage of relatively recently created social niches by assuming the role of culture broker or cultural interpreter or both. Because of the complexity of existing social and political systems, such niches allow certain members of the population to manipulate them by changing categories expediently. Those social categories may be understood as originating with colonial structural arrangements (see, e.g., Jean Comaroff 1985; John and Jean Comaroff 1992; Gordon 1992). While much of this study deals with the ambivalent role of mixedbloods in Bennett County, it is important to note that the complexity of imposed bureaucratic structures allows for manipulation and strategizing by all members of the population, in their own style (see Royce 1982).

This sociocultural study also is concerned with categories of identity as they were originally cast, and are still being played out, in a rural county and in state and national contexts. It illustrates the ways in which United States federal policies brought Oglala Lakotas, and their neighbors, to think of themselves in racial terms, where, previously, a politically loaded classification by race had not necessarily existed. Such racialization ultimately was tied to the primary goals of acquiring Indian land and assimilating Indian people. In many cases, "successful" family members adopted the foreign concept of individualism, which, in turn, laid the foundation for the emergence of a new social category, thereby complicating existing family relationships. The category that came to be known as "mixedblood" is powerful because of its ability to maintain culturally fluid and structurally flexible positions in new historical, political, and economic situations but, more often than not, at the expense of violating existing kinship expectations (see Ella C. Deloria 1944).

This study proceeds from certain presuppositions about racialized or ethnicized social categories. Such categories are the means by which people are *perceived* to be grouped together; they are not necessarily invested with political capital and may be descriptive in the simplest sense. They are not "natural" groupings of people or expressions of "natural factions." They are phenomena unto themselves, not euphemisms for class. Race and ethnicity do not exist in a vacuum. They are *always* products of historical forces, defined and influenced from both inside and outside the group. Race and ethnicity are more often not the products of sociocultural collisions but, rather, of collusion through the interactions of people at the "margins." Dynamics surrounding the formation of racial or ethnic groups often open possibilities for negotiations of identities in a social space that is not "this or that," but "both or neither." Such spaces may be occupied by "culture brokers" – cultural translators – who, because of their positions in the social system, are viewed as "other" by the very groups that they may be attempting to bridge. Their power actually may derive from their innate "otherness" and their ability simultaneously to access, identify with, and reinterpret symbols of both groups.

Despite academic discussions concerning the arbitrariness of categorization of people in terms of race, ethnicity, or class, such categories gain substance – are normalized – through decades of interactions between groups of people. Their recognition of difference is played out in myriad ways and is unique to each local situation – merely variations on a theme – indicating that, in Bennett County, for example, there is no final decision or ultimate identity. But in that ambiguous and often shifting difference, one discovers a commonality – a linkage – that binds diverse groups together into an unexpected unity. Through a locally negotiated social reality that makes sense in their everyday lives, a region of diverse "others" may become a region of "insiders" in the face of outside interference.

This study is organized in a manner that will, first and foremost, enable readers to peek over my shoulder as I observe in some detail several ethnographic "snapshots" taken from the flow of daily interactions. Daily life in Bennett County is generally taken up by the everyday tasks of earning a living. Farmers and ranchers work in their fields and tend to their animals, merchants order inventory and stock their shelves, teachers plan and teach classes, and health workers in the county hospital, nursing home, and clinic offer aid to the infirm. Elderly residents, particularly the women, busy themselves with quilting and making other treasured heirlooms for their families, for exhibit at the county fair, or for sale at the craft store on Main Street. There is also time for chatting with neighbors and catching up on gossip. Beyond the usual family problems and everyday economic and political concerns that always take center stage, life is typically unhurried and unproblematic. However, most of the narrative snapshots that I have chosen do not highlight those more or less uneventful daily community routines, but rather stand out as extraordinary moments reflecting a community in crisis.

The decision to describe and analyze the more unusual events that occurred during my stay was not made in the interest of depicting a community at its

3. Local handcrafts for sale

worst, but rather in the interest of using crisis situations to reveal the often masked divisions between groups of socially affiliated individuals. In unusual times of undeniable discord, community members are forced to articulate their social identities in very explicit and deliberate ways. These ethnographic snapshots serve to highlight problematic identities that may escape the parameters of the reifying labels of mixedblood, fullblood, and white in everyday lived experience. Certain snapshots are contemporary and based on firsthand observations; others have emerged from primary archival sources. They are not introduced in chronological order because chronology is not always useful in examining symbols that underlie social behavior and have been invested and reinvested with meaning. However, they will be presented in temporal order in the final chapter as an aid in discerning how contemporary local attitudes are intimately linked with historical events and policies, and how events previous may lead to expectations of those future.

The power of symbols as markers of identity is nowhere more clearly articulated than in ritual, which Victor Turner (1967:19) defines as "prescribed formal behavior" outside the routine of daily life. He writes: "I came to see performances of ritual as distinct phases in the social process whereby groups became adjusted to internal changes and adapted to their external environment. From

4. Lakota woman hand crafting a star quilt

this standpoint the ritual symbol becomes a factor in social action, a positive force in an activity field. The symbol becomes associated with human interests, purposes, ends, and means . . . The structure and properties of a symbol become those of a dynamic entity, at least within its appropriate context of action" (Turner 1967:20). Symbols are invested with meaning by participants and observers, and are multivocal and polysemic. Simply stated, they speak to people in many ways and may mean different things to different people, and they are always dependent on context and intention. Although many of the narrative snapshots depicted here are not recurring rituals such as church services or organized state events, they are acted out as public rituals nonetheless, reflecting certain continuities based on historical events and played out in public behaviors, whether scripted or contemporaneous.

The notion of casting local events in terms of discrete snapshots came about as I realized that the public events and secular rituals that I observed were meant to be positioned tableaux of idealized social relations in Bennett County. I intend each snapshot to be a moment out of time – a synchronic slice of life – purposefully lifted from history's course to enable the reader to develop a sense of each player's or group's significance and role in several community interactions. Assumptions about the character of the place are easier to make

5. Women making a holiday apple strudel from scratch

when the snapshots are viewed as discrete statements about identity in Bennett County in certain social contexts. When initially seen as one would view photos scattered on the floor, rather than chronologically arranged in a photo album, it is possible to enjoy a different perspective, one that allows for observation of each detail. But each snapshot having been viewed, it will be returned to an historical frame to more fully address the symbolic meanings behind the labels "mixedblood," "fullblood," and "white." In addition, it will be possible to interpret the processes of labeling as technologies of domination and their perhaps unintended consequences – manipulation of those same artificial social categories by local residents in different ways in different contexts.

Chapter 2 begins with narrative ethnographic snapshots of several events that occurred in conjunction with the 1996 Bennett County High School homecoming weekend and illustrates a secular community ceremony that harkens back to a romanticized, and contested, historical identity. Mirroring the national debate concerning the use of negatively depicted Indian mascots, that longstanding social event has drawn criticism from certain factions of Lakota people, both in Bennett County and at the national level. Predictable community relations are confounded when overlapping social fields, each with its own political agenda and backed up by its own interpretation of history, come together in Bennett County. This chapter sets the historical setting and focuses primarily on the land that had been, and some residents argue still is, a portion of the Pine Ridge Indian Reservation. It considers several acts of federal legislation that have affected treaty guarantees negotiated prior to the Dawes Act (General Allotment Act) of 1887, as well as other agreements and legislative acts that led to the further diminishment of the Oglala Lakota Sioux (ost) tribal lands and estate.

Chapter 3 examines the social self as expressed through racialized social categories and teases out cultural differences in Lakota and American reckonings of kinship and understandings of land. Those conceptualizations of kinship and land are then rewoven and are shown to form the bases for identity. A snapshot of the shooting of a local Lakota man by a non-Indian acquaintance illustrates the problem of the "outsider" in local events and how, in times of crisis, the impulse to racialize disputes lies just beneath the surface of everyday Bennett County life.

Chapter 4 addresses legal selves and begins with a brief overview of federal Indian laws concerning issues relevant to this study – land and blood. Excerpts of an interview with a deputy attorney general of South Dakota, himself a lifelong resident of Bennett County, point out the problem of federal Indian law in counties that contain a mixture of privately owned and tribally controlled land. Tribal, county, and state law enforcement officers discuss problems that are unique to counties with checkerboard jurisdiction.

The study concludes with a final set of snapshots in which "outsiders" play no significant roles, and provides further analysis of the snapshots, offering an explanation of identity in Bennett County that considers, and then incorporates, local social and cultural factors in historical context.

TWO

Bennett County High School Homecoming, 1996

Sensing places, men and women become sharply aware of the complex attachments that link them to features of the physical world. Sensing places, they dwell, as it were, on aspects of dwelling. Persons thus involved may also dwell on aspects of themselves, on sides and corners of their own evolving identities. For the self-conscious experience of place is invariably a product and expression of the self whose experience it is, and therefore, unavoidably, the nature of experience (its intentional thrust, its substantive content, its affective tones and colorings) is shaped at every turn by the personal and social biography of the one who sustains it. BASSO 1996:54–55

HOMECOMING SNAPSHOTS

In a small town, it is not uncommon for everyone to come together for sporting events, and Bennett County is not unusual in that respect. Local people are active in bowling and softball leagues and in golf, either as participants or as spectators. They spend summer evenings in Martin's city park, sitting in the bleachers of the baseball diamond, gossiping, discussing cattle and wheat prices, and enjoying a relaxing moment away from the daily routine. In sporting contests, neighbors' desires are simple: friendly competition and "bragging rights" over a cool beverage later on.

In contrast to this friendly intracommunity competition, high school athletics unite the community in the face of a "common enemy" – the rival team. At school games, the home team can demonstrate the support of their families and friends, who represent a unified common territory. The rival team will usually be accompanied by a few diehard supporters, representing a definite minority. In Martin, where pickups, vans, and cars are allowed to park on a bluff behind the visitors' bleachers and behind one of the Bennett County High School's goal posts, the noise level is significant. Radios are tuned to the local station and horns blare whenever the Bennett County team scores. Horns also blare when the visiting team scores, because fans are willing to drive many miles to support their teams, even in miserable weather. County rivalries are renowned, especially between Bennett County High School and teams from the neighboring counties, among which are Pine Ridge Reservation (Shannon County and part of Jackson County, once known as Washabaugh County) and Rosebud Reservation (Todd County).

High school teams symbolize a community's ability to unite and compete against outsiders. In Bennett County, neighbors take a break from personal boundary maintenance by participating together both on the field and in the stands in a show of positive community identity. Their common goal is to cheer the home team on to victory and display community pride.

The relevant issue here lies in the symbol adopted by the Bennett County High School teams, the Warriors and the Lady Warriors. Their logo is a tasteful representation of an Indian warrior, seen in profile, wearing a Plains Indian headdress of eagle feathers. This logo bears no resemblance to those of certain professional sporting teams, since it does not portray negatively perceived racial characteristics, but rather attempts to capture a sense of pride, courage, and ability in battle. Like all symbols, this logo is a vacant sign until invested with meaning. To the people it represents, it is a unifying symbol, while opponents assign alternate interpretations.

During my stay, certain local fullbloods expressed concern that such representations are inappropriate, since they consider the Warrior imagery to be their own. The resulting debate is more than a struggle for a symbol. It is a contest expressed in racial terms and also in the vernacular of property rights. The following series of ethnographic snapshots illustrates the power that the Warrior symbol holds for different groups of community members, as well as for people residing outside that social field. I present the snapshots descriptively so that the reader can see them as I did. After the narrative descriptions, I discuss how Bennett County was established, and how historical factors added significant and multivalent meanings to what could have been just another homecoming weekend.

The March, Thursday Afternoon

Coming down Main Street from the west, and borne by a Lakota man, was the American Indian Movement flag. The flag – blue, yellow, green, and red, with the silhouette of an Indian man wearing two black eagle feathers – snapped smartly in the plains wind. The group following the flag was about one hundred strong and was made up of men, women, and children from every stage of life. There were residents of Bennett County and Pine Ridge Reservation, and a few non-Indian teachers and students from Oglala Lakota College and from

6. Demonstrators led by a woman in Lakota regalia

Minnesota, where the local woman in buckskin who walked in front of the procession was a student. The singing of a Lakota drum group bearing their drum along in the center of the procession could be clearly heard; the other marchers were silent.

Main Street was particularly quiet. A few people ventured out of stores for a fleeting glimpse of the goings-on, but, for the most part, the only witnesses along the street were Bennett County and tribal police officers who were blocking traffic for the marchers, and me. I wanted only to watch this march and the reactions to it from my "objective" stance on the curb as an ethnographer with no opinion, but when the woman who months before had extended her family to include me, and who refers to me as her sister, motioned me over to walk with her grandchildren, I did not refuse.

We walked to the park, where a "feed" (feast) of soup, fry bread, *wóžapi* 'berry pudding', Jello, beautifully decorated sheet cakes, and coffee awaited the marchers and anyone else who wanted to come and hear Lakota grievances concerning the use of warrior symbolism in the homecoming ceremony. A speaker system borrowed from KILI radio station ("The Voice of the Lakota Nation") in Pine Ridge sat on a picnic table, ready to broadcast the event and to document it for their archives. Already, many cars and pickups were at the

7. Anti-Warrior homecoming march

park. Many of the "elderlies" and their families had come for dinner regardless of whether they agreed with the agenda, and the usual faces were there waiting to share a community meal and catch up on gossip. But they also had come to listen. I saw no non-Indians, except for those married to Lakotas, and a few professors from Oglala Lakota College, some of whom were visiting professors from back east, and who had marched along. I was surprised that not more community members had come to hear what the group had to say.

The young woman in buckskin took the microphone and discussed her feeling: the homecoming was a sacrilege, using Indian symbolism without really knowing anything about it. While her speech was impassioned, some individuals in the Indian community of Bennett County believed that this woman had raised all the fuss because neither she nor her twin sister had been nominated for Warrior Princess the year before. She had been actively involved in school activities during her high school career, had been a cheerleader, and had helped previous homecoming committees secure Lakota star quilts for the football team to wear in the homecoming ceremony. Many wondered why she was now making such a big deal of the whole affair.

The year before, officials from the American Indian Movement (AIM) had, in a written letter, given her complete support, promising to be in Martin in force if Bennett County did not cease and desist using Indian imagery and symbolism in an unauthorized secular manner. One local Lakota man had told me months before that AIM would not waste time and resources on Bennett County because it was "small potatoes"; his assessment proved to be correct. An Oglala Lakota College student representative of AIM read a note stating that, while AIM was in complete support of the demonstration, circumstances did not permit them to be at the homecoming that year. A letter of support from jailed AIM activist Leonard Peltier was also read to the audience, but ultimately the offended students would have to make their protest in their own words and in their own way.[1]

One of the speakers, from the Wanblee district of Pine Ridge, was an elderly woman in a burgundy dance shawl, herself a well respected member of the Grey Eagle Society (an influential organization of Lakota elders) and powerful spokeswoman for Lakota values (see fig. 8). She called for changes in the ceremony that would better reflect American values, suggesting that perhaps conspicuous displays of wealth – diamonds, gold, and tiaras – would be more appropriate. This was ironic, considering the pervasively marginal economic status of Bennett County ranchers, farmers, and merchants. As she spoke, some Lakota teenagers made a point of acting bored and attracting attention to themselves. But the elderly woman continued her remarks, ignoring them.

Several speakers rose to present arguments concerning what they considered to be institutionalized racist practices in Bennett County, from the treatment of Indian inmates in the county jail to the lack of opportunities other than for a few superior Indian athletes. I got the sense that this all amounted to preaching to the converted, since no county officials were there to hear these grievances. The futility of the exercise eloquently proved the marginalization and invisibility of the protestors in Martin. After the feed, knots of people drifted off to prepare for the homecoming ceremony that would take place in a couple of hours.

Coronation of Homecoming Royalty, Thursday Evening

Spectators usually crowd shoulder to shoulder in metal folding chairs behind those reserved for student athletes soon to be seated in positions of honor directly in front of the stage.[2] Silvery stars decorate the blue stage curtain, and a canvas tipi, painted with horse, buffalo, eagle, and sun images, sits on the stage. Toward the center of the stage is a pile of logs to be "lit" with a bulb wired to the backside, suggesting a campfire. The large purple and gold banner depicting an Indian with an eagle-feathered headdress and reading "Home of the WARRIORS" hangs on the front of the stage. This was a gift from the Class of 1981.

8. An elder speaks of traditional Lakota values

I surveyed the crowd and recognized that in some cases, four generations of family members were represented. Years of intermarriage have blurred cultural and phenotypical boundaries, but identity politics continue to divide the county, particularly in times of social crisis. Homecoming was usually a time to put those divisions aside, at least for that one special evening, but in 1996, there were many empty seats.

I was unaware of the demonstrators silently making their way into the auditorium until derogatory comments from adult non-Indian and some mixed-blood community members behind me drew my attention to them. They filed past the high school principal, county sheriff, deputies, and state highway patrol officers to form a circle separating audience from participants. Scruffy demonstrators, many of the younger ones dressed in baggy jeans and "gang colors," remained silent as they held placards referring to symbols, mascots, and justice. Some local residents shouted epithets like "Who did you get to print them signs?" implying either that the demonstrators were too uneducated to produce them themselves, or that only an outsider would have produced them. A reporter for *Indian Country Today* appeared to be in close contact with the demonstrators. I asked a photographer from that newspaper later about his role in the demonstration and was told obliquely that at homecoming

9. The homecoming site, 1996

the previous year, someone from Bennett County had sweetened his gas tank with sugar.

For the most part, the demonstrators were silent as the student athletes filed into their seats. I noticed that compromises already negotiated by the student council, school superintendent, and tribal members who had contested aspects of the ceremony for several years were being carried out as agreed. Following a smaller protest the previous year, it had been agreed that the athletes would not process to or sit on the stage in Lakota star quilts, have their faces painted with "war paint," or wear feathers in their hair. This compromise exempted the "Big Chief," however, who was still allowed to wear a feathered headdress. This represented a sharp change from earlier years, when elaborate outfits were loaned to the candidates for homecoming royalty by the Red Cloud family and other prominent leaders from Pine Ridge Reservation.

The first several rows of folding chairs had been reserved for other student athletes, whose eyes, wide with fear, searched for the faces of their parents – someone familiar – as commotion in the auditorium escalated. They displayed no challenging eye contact toward the demonstrators, whose faces wore expressions ranging from simply dour to overtly confrontational. The students tried to ignore them, but I had the sense that they were being forced to decide their racial affiliation then and there. One fullblood cheerleader chose to side with the high school in this dispute, but it was painful for her to do so. Seeds of yet another generation of potential racial discord were being scattered on soil that the disruption had ploughed and readied.

Traditionally, when each Warrior Princess candidate entered the gym on her escort's arm, the main lights would be turned off and a single spotlight focused on the pair, who would process solemnly to the stage as the principal announced the achievements of each candidate and her escort. Tonight, however, lights remained fully lit, thus removing one element of ritual enactment and interfering with the crowd's expectation of continuity. On this night, princess candidates wore unadorned buckskin dresses and simple headbands. Escorts wore their football jerseys and jeans without star quilts, blankets, or face paint. They looked frightened but remained solemnly composed, as their roles demanded. Early in the procession, demonstrators stood stoically while Bennett County supporters went wild with cheers and applause.

When each couple arrived at the stairs leading to the stage, they found a middle-aged Lakota woman and a young girl, holding hands to block the way. The couples were forced to halt, and only after establishing eye contact were they allowed to pass. It appeared that passage was denied longer and longer with each couple. Since the boys were visibly uncomfortable in asking permission to pass and hesitant to break the chain, the sheriff intervened by demanding that the woman and child quit obstructing the procession. They unclasped their hands but still attempted to make eye contact with each passing couple.

When Big Chief took his place in the procession, one of the protestors in front of me angrily yelled, "Take it off!" referring to the feathered headdress that he wore. People behind me were shouting, "If you don't like it, leave!" and "Go home where you belong!" Counter shouts of "Justice for one and justice for all!" resounded through the auditorium, drowning out the announcer and robbing candidates of public recognition of the considerable achievements of their high school careers. Shouts were becoming angrier and the stress on students' faces even more pronounced. Mixedblood candidates and their escorts drew especially large rounds of applause from county supporters.

By the time the last pair took the stage, the shouts and cheers had grown deafening. At this point, the protestors moved *en masse* into the open space between the athletes and the stage, a large American Indian Movement banner insinuating itself as the predominant symbol (see Firth 1973:328–67 on flag symbolism). Chaos ensued as a traditional Lakota drum group sang and the crowd attempted to drown them out with their own school pep song. Law enforcement officers entered the demonstrators' space and escorted the Lakota drum group out, to cheers from the bleachers and boos from the protestors and their supporters.

In the midst of that chaos, "Little Chief" was attempting to choose the Princess, circling the candidates, who were seated on the stage around the artificial fire. No one could hear the song that the Princess candidates sang, not only because of shouts and counter shouts, but because the girls traditionally sang a very soft *a cappella*. Little Chief was one of the roles that had been significantly altered from previous years, when he was portrayed as a medicine man. There had been severe criticism from the Lakota community that his dance was an insulting parody of Lakota traditional dance, as well as of the medicine man's significant role in Lakota life. One of the local Lakotas, himself a graduate of Bennett County High School and recognized as the best powwow dancer in the region, had taught this year's Little Chief (a non-Indian) a few moves. His dance, while in need of improvement, was certainly not the parody that it had been the year before.

This year's selection process was still problematic because of the way that Little Chief chose a suitable Warrior Princess for the Big Chief. He danced around the semicircle of young women, touching their hair, assessing their heft by raising each by her elbows from behind, and looking into their mouths as if to examine their teeth. Many later noted that if not racist, this part of the ceremony was definitely sexist, and in no way reflected the ways in which a Lakota man would assess a woman's value. Finally, Little Chief declared his choice. No one was surprised that the resulting couple, elected by the students, were the most phenotypically "Indian" mixedbloods, and their popularity and considerable high school accomplishments were eclipsed by their phenotype. Little Chief provided balance by being non-Indian. The group stood on the stage as a highly visible multivalent symbol of what was supposed to be Bennett County's unique identity. The chanting demonstrators filed down the center aisle and out of the building.

From the back of the gym, the young local woman in buckskin who had begun protesting the ceremony the previous year, together with several others, returned to the building and positioned their backs to the stage. I read the lips of the woman in buckskin as she whispered urgently under her breath in a frightened way to the girl beside her, "Come in everybody!" She was extremely afraid, but was putting up a good front. Then from the rear of the hall came "war whoops" and ululations. The protestors joined the small group, once again interrupting the ceremony with chants for justice.

Following the coronation, the royalty and athletes were unceremoniously hustled down the stairs behind the stage without the usual finale of recessing through applauding, moist-eyed relatives. Plans were in place to use that route because the basement door could be locked to protect them from any violence that might occur. The audience simply filed out, bringing the community tradition to a very inelegant end. No one seemed quite sure what to do and many

10. Protestors return to the stage

were silently shaking their heads as they left. One non-Indian woman who was married to a fullblood man cradled their mixedblood baby and wept quietly.

The Bonfire, Thursday Night

I wondered how the bonfire would go this year. The year before, the young woman who "caused the uproar" had read letters from AIM officials stating that if the Bennett County Warriors continued negative stereotypical representations, they would come in force to protest. I recalled the scene vividly. The girl and her supporters, numbering perhaps sixty, stood on the gentle hillside overlooking the crowd that had gathered to celebrate. Below them, on the running track, stood the Warrior team, Big Chief, Little Chief, and the Warrior Princess and her court, behind whom were gathered their families and other community members. I was struck by the fact that the Big Chief, Little Chief, and most of the football team had turned their backs to the woman who was reading her demands in a clear and articulate manner, using direct but not inflammatory language. The Warrior Princess and the other young women were more polite and listened to what was said. Turning backs seemed to be a way of making the woman with the complaint feel invisible; all the more so for the fact that she had been a cheerleader for that team.

But this year, after being hustled protectively out of the gym, the Bennett County Warriors gathered at the edge of the outdoor running track that circles the high school football field. From there they could look up the hill toward two massive metal frames bearing oil-soaked rags, forming the Bennett County initials. As a precaution, homecoming royalty and their court attended in street clothes instead of Lakota regalia, which had been the practice in the past. The field was dimly lit as I stood with the team and other high school students, proud parents and siblings, and vocal community supporters. Despite palpable tension, I heard no racist comments from players cheering themselves on to victory in the forthcoming game – even though they were also cheering themselves on to maintain control of the Warrior symbol.

Then a player gestured urgently toward a spot just to the right of the unlit bonfire on the rise where the young woman, dressed in traditional Lakota garb of white fringed buckskin with lavish hand-stitched beadwork, led a group of silent protestors to the edge of the precipice. An American Indian Movement banner again snapped briskly above them in the chilly evening breeze, and the sound of a drum rolled down the hill toward the field.

Suddenly I felt transported back over one hundred years in time. It took a moment to realize that the surrealistic montage coming to life before me was real. Time slowed to a virtual standstill as I was transformed into an extra in one of the oldtime Westerns that I had seen as a child. Backlit by the lights of the high school beyond my range of vision, the figures on the hill seemed silhouetted instead by one of Hollywood's famous setting suns. "Damn! The Indians have snuck up on us again! Circle the wagons, men. It's us against them!" The words were in my mind, and only there.

It seemed that I was no longer in Bennett County. I felt an ominous tension embedded in my own consciousness from years of Western movies, novels, and songs. I filled the mythical role of newcomer – outsider – circled by the "hostiles," and was excruciatingly aware of the depths of my own cultural conditioning as I experienced on a visceral level what my intellect had long known. Myths can be very real. The scene caused an unreconcilable muddle where "fight-or-flight" adrenalin rush met an awesome sense of peace as if I had already lived through this moment and knew the outcome.

Just as suddenly, this "objective" observer was back, taking in the scene as the protestors attempted once again to get between Bennett County and its symbols by surrounding the huge letters as they were set afire, but the heat, danger, and a few words from local volunteer firefighters deterred them. While the attempt to co-opt that community symbol failed, the division of the people on the hill was itself symbolic of Bennett County relations. Community members stood on the left facing the blazing letters; protestors, most of whom live out of the county on the neighboring Pine Ridge Indian Reservation, stood on the right, with a discernable strip of bare land between them. For the most part, Bennett County residents pretended to ignore the protestors, but were prepared for confrontation.

The bonfire was extinguished amid unearthly and turbulent surges of steam, and the Bennett County Warriors and their families and friends simply wandered off toward their cars on Main Street, not even waiting for the embers to die. The protestors descended the hill to the football field, formed a large circle, and prayed to *Thųkáśila* 'Grandfather; the Great Spirit', vowing to return next year in an even more effective demonstration. The woman standing in the center praised the protestors for their commitment to Lakota tradition, saying that they should be proud for speaking what they believe in a good way. When an anonymous hand at the high school switched off the solitary fieldlight, they, too, wandered back up the hill toward Main Street.

I stayed for awhile to reflect on the event. In hindsight, the protest was vocal but nonviolent, and the town residents were remarkable in their restraint. They felt violated and invaded by "outsiders" and yet were not provoked into physical confrontations. The obvious implication of the protest was that local Indian people should join in, meaning anguish for those caught in the middle of conflicting identites. Some were both fullbloods *and* Bennett County Warriors. The formal protest held earlier in the public park was equally restrained, but because no local non-Indians or mixedbloods, and only a few Lakotas who lived in a tribal housing project in the county, attended, no community outreach was achieved, no dialogue established. The protestors were shunned by the community, and that was no accident. Lines had been drawn in the shifting sand.

It should be noted that, while the outward appearance was one of indifference, many mixedbloods and non-Indians had, in fact, been deputized to keep watch over the homecoming events. They were furnished with two-way radios and were a ubiquitous, if intentionally invisible presence. They were determined to control any negative situation instigated by outsiders. At the end of the evening, a few community agitators from the Lakota HUD cluster were menacing some high school students who were capping off the evening by cruising Main Street. One young local Lakota was particularly aggressive, but as a clergywoman and I watched with a man who had been deputized, it was clear that the guardian would not jump into the fray prematurely. He was simply vigilant, observing.

Like a flock of geese spooked from a field, the agitators suddenly took off on a run toward the highway. The three of us jumped into the deputized mixedblood's van and followed. In front of the firehouse, groups of teenagers had faced off, standing in rows and exchanging fighting words. There were many other vigilantes, some deputized, some not, and all remained in their cars, ready to rush into the fray should a fight break out. The potentially violent situation finally ended when the high school students left in groups.

My roles as observer and reluctant participant in the AIM march, witness to the homecoming coronation and bonfire, and potential vigilante confirmed that this was an unusual day indeed for Bennett County. Not so unusual, though, that the local population could not read its signs and risks and be prepared.

The Homecoming Parade, Saturday Afternoon

It seemed as though almost everyone in town participated in the 1996 homecoming parade on Main Street, although there were enough small groups of appreciative spectators to make the celebration an unintimidating, well-received social event. Compared to that of the previous year, this parade was the local equivalent of a Cecil B. DeMille production. Spectators expressed delight that this part of homecoming week, coupled with the overwhelming victory of the football team, was an unqualified, and apparently uncontested, success. A few grim-faced AIM supporters stood on the periphery with their arms folded across their chests and carefully observed the goings on, but for the most part, the crowd expressed its jubilation at the demonstration of county pride through enthusiastic hoots and applause. The success of the event seemed important for the elementary and high school students riding on various floats and marching in rows, shoulder to shoulder.

The day was chilly but sunny, with only a few puffy clouds scudding across the sky. I stood with an elderly Lakota friend who had been a teacher in small one-room schools and who delighted in pointing out the grammar and spelling mistakes on the banners that had been drawn and lettered by the elementary school students. "My students would *never* have made those silly mistakes, and their handwriting would have been far superior," she commented. The feeling of excitement and exuberance among the spectators was palpable, if perhaps slightly exaggerated.

It was important that the breach in community relations be addressed and the best community face put forth, at any cost. Floats groaning under their burdens of fullblood, mixedblood, and white elementary and high school students filed by. Candy was flung from the floats to the younger children lined up at the curbs, resulting in good-natured elbowing and scuffles to grab as much as possible to stuff into mouths and bulging pockets. Fire engines from local and nearby communities sounded their impressive sirens and caused us to cover our ears for protection; the dogs and puppies in attendance howled like coyotes in response. This festive display of solidarity meant even more to those

11. County kids on parade

on the sidelines because it could bring closure to the crisis brought on by the unsettled and contested homecoming ceremony a couple of days before.

The parade came off without a hitch. It expressed a remarkable and seamless community pride in the football team, the homecoming royalty (dressed not in buckskin outfits, but rather in street clothes), and the community itself. Bennett County had survived the worst; now the "real" community could be seen and applauded. No one broke ranks – Indian and white banded together in a reflection of yet another crisis overcome.

IDENTITIES IN HISTORICAL PERSPECTIVE

This section provides a fuller context for understanding relations between full-bloods, mixedbloods, and whites in Bennett County. The historical background of this region will enable the reader to revisit the homecoming snapshots and view them in a different way, taking into account the complex histories of tribal and non-Indian perceptions concerning early federal policies that still color community relations. Although such social dramas are played out at the contemporary regional level, "outsiders" from differing social fields have always had an impact that, more often than not, sets the stage for local struggles over symbolic – and physical – territory and identities.

12. Homecoming royalty in 1996 parade

Blending Land and Blood

Dakota Territory was one small portion of the land acquired by the United States from France for three cents an acre in the 1803 Louisiana Purchase. Lewis and Clark explored the region on the orders of President Thomas Jefferson in an expedition that began the following year, with the mandate of improving relations with Indian tribes in order to secure the continuation of the profitable fur trade. A second goal was to locate a navigable river leading to the western coast. News from the expedition fueled the ambitions of Americans desiring to move west, some looking to settle on small farms, others hoping to build shining "cities on the hill," and still others seeking, first and foremost, to be free of excessive governmental control. It was not until 1849 that full-fledged Western expansion brought settlers across the plains. However, previous encounters with primarily French and Scotch-Irish trappers and traders had already led to intercultural trade and personal relationships between European men and Indian women.

With the conclusion of the American Civil War in 1865, the nation turned its attention to ending, once and for all, the Indian Wars still being fought on the frontier. The defeat of General George Armstrong Custer at the Battle of the Little Bighorn in June of 1876 caused an enraged Eastern population to react strongly, but not in unison. Some preferred a military solution, while others argued that Indians should be settled on reservations where they could live unmolested by the intrusions of non-Indian traders, liquor salesmen, and speculators attempting to defraud them of their land. Since the expense of the Civil War had greatly diminished treasury funds and the cost of fighting Indian wars continued to escalate, those preferring reservations won out. In the Treaty of 1868, the entire West River country of South Dakota and the eastern half of what was to become Wyoming was set aside as reservation and hunting land for the Sioux (Kappler 1904:998–1007). This remote area was tucked far enough away from major population centers to render Lakotas invisible to those who were filled with entrepreneurial hopes of building another New York or Chicago on the prairie (Nelson 1986). Lakotas were to be "directed" in proper farming skills by Indian agents and "civilized" through exposure to Christian Bibles, brought to them by Roman Catholic and Protestant missionaries; some of the more successful missionaries were Indian men who had converted to one brand of Christianity or another. Such acculturative processes were but the prelude to the more assimilative processes that followed, and they worked in tandem to "civilize" the tribes.

Two provisions of Article 6 of the 1868 treaty underlie contemporary problems of land tenure and identity in Bennett County. First, individuals who were heads of families (including non-Indian men married to Indian women at the time of signing) could choose allotments of up to 320 acres if they wished to take up farming. This land would then be held in severalty as long as it continued to be cultivated. In essence, the treaty enabled non-Indian men well-versed in western understandings of land to become "Indian" in terms of access to land, annuities, health, and education benefits, and future Indian programs. Second came the problem of fractionated allotments. The same article provided that "the United States may pass such laws on the subject of alienation and descent of property between the Indians and their descendants as may be thought proper" (Kappler 1904:1000). Later, "proper" statutory actions concerning Indian land and heirship contributed to a further diminution of Indian land, since land was often divided among hundreds of heirs. It was reported that one heir, for example, "possessed equities in numerous allotments, up to the number of hundreds" (Collier, quoted in Getches and Wilkinson 1986:117). Since these equities were often insignificant in size, sometimes measured in inches, they could not be used for farming or ranching and they did not bring income to the heirs. To make matters worse, such parcels could be sold only with the agreement of all the heirs, a unanimity rarely achieved. The problem of fractionated allotments was not remedied until the Indian Land Consolidation Act of 1982 (Prucha 1990:300).

Two conceptual formulations of the "Indian Problem" existed side by side in the late nineteenth century. Zealous reformers, most of whom lived on the east coast far from the frontier, and other "friends of the Indian" sought to "elevate and civilize savages" by teaching them "useful" arts. In contrast, others advocated the forceful corralling of Indians onto reservations out of sight of the tide of western settlers and those passing through the territory to find their fortune in the gold mines farther west. Either way, life was changing rapidly for Lakota people who, up until a few years before, had lived a successful and socially integrated nomadic lifestyle. Some of the reformers' assimilative solutions, intended to help Indians, actually aggravated the "Indian Problem" because of the reformers' naive and unexamined ethnocentric notions (Hoxie 1984). According to one historian, "even the friends of the Indian who sought to have him safely isolated on reservation knew that American expansionism, technology and racial ideology would reduce the Indian to a pitiful remnant of a once proud and flourishing people" (Blinderman 1978:17). By and large, reformers believed that they were sympathetic to the plight of the Indians and knew the proper ways to bring them to economic prosperity. Unfortunately, and despite those intentions, many significant cultural differences escaped their attention.

The General Allotment Act, also called the Dawes Act, was adopted on February 2, 1887, but not without dissent (Prucha 1990:171–74). Senator Henry M. Teller of Colorado had decried an earlier proposal to allot Indian land as a "bill to despoil the Indians of their lands and to make them vagabonds on the face of the earth" (Otis 1973:18). Displaying both an understanding of cultural difference and a prophetic insight into subsequent events, he later argued that, "if I stand alone in the Senate, I want to put upon the record my prophecy in this matter, that when 30 or 40 years shall have passed and these Indians shall have parted with their title, they will curse the hand that was raised professedly in their defense . . . and if the people who are clamoring for it understood Indian character, and Indian laws, and Indian morals, and Indian religion, they would not be here clamoring for this at all" (Otis 1973:18). The initial purpose of allotting land to individual Indians may have been to protect them, but by the end of the nineteenth century the policy became a tool to break up tribal social structure and land holdings and a device for assimilating Indians into the dominant culture (Getches and Wilkinson 1986:111). President Theodore Roosevelt, himself an advocate of westward expansion and a speedy solution to the Indian Problem, referred to allotment policies as "a mighty pulverizing engine" (quoted in Getches and Wilkinson 1986:111) that would rapidly break down communal control of land and place it in the hands of individuals. Those individuals, of course, would be taxpayers.

The chief provisions of the act itself were: (1) a grant of one-quarter section (160 acres) to the head of each family, one-eighth section (80 acres) to each single person over eighteen years old and to orphans under eighteen years old, and one-sixteenth section (40 acres) to single persons under eighteen years of age at the date of the order; (2) a fee patent issued to each allottee, but held in trust for twenty-five years, during which time the land could not be alienated or encumbered; (3) a period of four years for Indians to make their selections, after which, agents of the Secretary of the Interior would select land for them; and (4) the conferral of U.S. citizenship upon allottees and any other Indians who severed tribal ties and adopted "the habits of civilized life" (see full text in Prucha 1990:171–74).

Conferral of citizenship was an important provision of the act. It applied to two classes of Indians – those who received allotments, and those others who earlier had voluntarily taken up "civilized ways." However, the Burke Act of 1906 (Prucha 1990:207) amended the Dawes Act regarding the first of these classes. The Burke Act was intended to protect Indians from "the vices of non-Indian society by keeping [them] under federal supervision as long as necessary," except in cases when the allottee could be deemed competent (McDonnell 1991:88). In those latter cases, a fee patent (deed) would be issued. Here again, implementation of policy departed from expressed intent, as the act opened the way for agents to certify competency for expediency's sake, despite the protests of Indians who did not wish to accept the terms of allotment.

Early Lakota signers of negotiated treaties and agreements did not understand that western legal traditions allow for statutory amendments and even reversals of previous laws (see Deloria and DeMallie 1999, 1:6–8). In 1889, when agents of the federal government came to explain further planned diminution of Sioux land through the breaking up of the Great Sioux Reservation, Lakota spokesmen argued vehemently against such plans, noting the results of earlier treaty provisions for Sioux tribes. The Act to Divide the Great Sioux Reservation [25 Stat. 888] (which was fully entitled "An act to divide a portion of the reservation of the Sioux Nations of Indians in Dakota into separate reservations and to secure the relinquishment of the Indian title to the remainder, and for other purposes"), did serve several purposes. Those most relevant to this study include the division and reduction of the reservation and "protection" from further intrusions of non-Indians, who had streamed into the area in defiance of the Treaty of 1868. This act also facilitated the implementation of the allotment process on the divided and greatly reduced Sioux reservations.

In the final analysis, as one opponent of the Dawes Act had prophesied: "the primary effect of the Allotment Act was a precipitous decline in the total amount of Indian-held land, from 138 million acres in 1887 to 48 million in

1934. Of the 48 million acres that remained, some 20 million were desert or semi-desert [as in Pine Ridge] . . . Allottees who received patents after 25 years found themselves subject to state property taxation, and many forced sales resulted from non-payment" (Canby 1988:21; for an economist's perspective on allotment policy, see Carlson 1981). Sioux legal scholars have argued that allotment policy "redirected the thrust of the federal-Indian relationship to that of property management," with all the attendant bureaucratic structures to manage Indian resources (Deloria and Lytle 1984:5). In addition to the increased presence of the federal government on reservations, allotment policy brought enormous pressures to bear upon Indians to renounce their tribal ties and become United States citizens. Of course, those new citizens might not have ready cash to pay their new taxes, with the result that some lost their land immediately.

Because individually owned land was a foreign concept to Lakotas, the imposition of the Dawes Act, combined with blood quantum rationales for severalty (see chapter 3), set the tone for the anticipated rapid assimilation of Pine Ridge Lakotas. That legislation was "the first comprehensive proposal to replace tribal consciousness with an understanding of the value of private property. The idea was not only to discourage native habits but to encourage Indians to accept the social and economic standards of white society" (McDonnell 1991:1). Lakotas were going to have to deal with the realities of life in the late nineteenth century and learn to think of themselves in terms of property ownership, lineal descent, and inheritance laws. Ella C. Deloria, an ethnographer and linguist who worked closely with Franz Boas, and herself a Yankton Sioux woman, sums it up elegantly:

> And it came, and without their asking for it – a totally different way of life, far-reaching in its influence, awful in its power, insistent in its demands. It came like a flood that nothing could stay. All in a day, it seemed, it had roiled the peacefulness of the Dakotas' lives, confused their minds, and given them but one choice – to conform to it, or else! And this it could force them to do because, by its very presence, it was even then making their way no longer feasible. [Deloria 1944:76–77]

Indians were not the only ones affected by federal policies concerning land. Ancestors of contemporary non-Indian ranchers and farmers were able to take advantage of inexpensive alternatives to overcrowded city life. Over a decade before the allotment of Indian land was formulated, Congress passed laws regarding the opening of the West to non-Indian settlement. The Homestead Act of 1862 was intended to be a remedy for cities plagued by overcrowding and unemployment; it would improve laborers' wages in the cities by encouraging, and then enabling, some people to leave them. For a small filing fee, the Homestead Act provided 160 acres of land to anyone (U.S. citizen or immigrant newcomer) who would agree to live on the land for five years and improve it. After six months, homesteaders were able to "prove up" (make the specified improvements) and buy the land for $1.25 per acre. More affluent individuals opted to buy land outright, as soon as possible, in order to mortgage it and buy other parcels from less successful homesteaders. The law was intended to guarantee independence to hardworking farmers, and Horace Greeley assessed it as "one of the most beneficent and vital reforms ever attempted in any age or clime – a reform calculated to diminish sensibly the number of paupers and idlers and increase the proportion of working, independent, self-subsisting farmers in the land evermore" (White 1991:143).

Other supporters believed that it "ensured a final realization of the old paired goals that had inspired the land system: a class of prosperous small farmers whose own prosperity fed the economic development of the nation" (White 1991:143). But the act also profited Eastern speculators with ready cash and time to wait for homesteaders, many unable to make a living in the harsh climate, to fail. According to Richard White, "in the Homestead Act, Congress above all expected the American future to duplicate the American past. Congress embedded the ideal of a 160-acre farm in the Homestead Act. It was an ideal more suited to the East than the West and more appropriate for the American past than the American future" (White 1991:142). By the time Bennett County was opened to non-Indian settlement in 1910, and, for that matter, when the Indians received their allotments, it was obvious that 160-acre plots were recipes for disaster in this part of the country. "Without irrigation, a quarter-section farm in the middle of the Great Plains . . . was not a ticket to independence but to starvation" (White 1991:142–43; see also U.S. Government 1936).

The Homestead Act differed from the Dawes Act in one significant way: after the homesteads were paid for (possibly after as little as six months), the land fell into the possession of homesteaders who then could sell it to speculators for a profit or mortgage it for funds to increase their own holdings. Such provisions did not exist in the Dawes Act or the later Burke Act, except when an Indian was deemed competent and had officially severed his tribal ties, or had them severed for him by the agent's practice of converting his land to deeded status without his petitioning for it. Even if they had had the desire, Lakotas had no legal opportunity to build large personal estates and all too often lost both their land and their identities that were so strongly rooted to it.

There was one particular humiliation that non-Indians did not have to endure: the official severing of tribal ties. This elaborate and highly ritualized ceremony was concocted by the Competency Commission, headed by James

McLaughlin, and symbolized an Indian's change in status from tribal member to American citizen. Secretary of the Interior Franklin K. Lane, when visiting the Yankton Reservation where the first such ceremony was to be held in 1916, noted with dismay that many of the Indian patentees had already made arrangements to sell their land. Nonetheless, the ceremony continued. According to Janet McDonnell (1991:95):

> During the ritual, each Indian who was to receive a fee patent and citizenship solemnly stepped from a teepee, and shot an arrow to signify that he was leaving behind his way of life. Moving forward slowly he placed his hands on a plow to demonstrate that he had chosen to live the farming life of a white man, with sweat and hard work. The secretary of the interior or other presiding official then handed the Indian a purse to remind him to save what he earned. Then with the secretary and the Indian holding the American flag, the Indian repeated these words: 'Foreasmuch as the President has said that I am worthy to be a citizen of the United States, I now promise this flag that I will give my hands, my head, and my heart to the doing of all that will make me a true American citizen.' To conclude the ceremony, the secretary pinned on the recipient a badge decorated with the American eagle and the national colors – the emblem of citizenship, which would remind the Indian always to act in a way that would make the flag proud.

Francis Paul Prucha notes that "the ceremonies were festive occasions and appeared to be appreciated by the Indians" (1984:881). At the time, many critics pointed out that "the patentees sold their lands, wasted the sale money, and ended up worse than before, but supporters of the program, although they admitted some evils in it, were convinced that fee patents and citizenship were the only road along which Indians could advance. Even Indians who lost their land gained valuable experience and learned a lesson in responsibility" (Prucha 1984:882).

The Opening and Secession of Bennett County

Bennett County was carved out of the Pine Ridge Indian Reservation in 1910 and formally organized two years later. It is bordered by the Pine Ridge (*Oglála Lakhóta*) Reservation to the north and west, the Rosebud Sioux (*Sicháǧu Lakhóta*) Reservation to the east, and the Nebraska state line to the south. It is a virtual jurisdictional island, and jurisdiction is complicated – and limited – because approximately one-third of the county remains "Indian Country." The term "Indian Country," defined in 1948, refers to federal jurisdiction over certain land within individual states, including land within Indian reservations (whether or not a patent has been issued), and rights-of-way through reservations (18 U.S.C. 1151). Federal jurisdiction also applies to "dependent Indian communities," whether within or outside the original or subsequently acquired reservation borders. The most pertinent definition for Bennett County is that federal jurisdiction extends to unextinguished Indian titles on all Indian allotments, including rights-of-way through them (see chapter 4). Many Lakotas still consider all but the city of Martin, the county seat and the only formally organized town in the county, to be reservation land (Wagoner 1998b).

From the outset, it was apparent that support for opening the county to general non-Indian homesteading would not be forthcoming from the fullbloods, who were in the majority in all reservation districts.[3] John R. Brennan, the superintending agent at Pine Ridge, expressed concern that the bill was premature, since only half of the slated 7,300 allotments had been completed by 1909 and the remainder would take at least two more years to complete. He observed that

> very few allotments have been made in the eastern part of the strip but it will be about all allotted next summer and after the work is finished in that part of the reservation there will not be a foot of good land, nothing but Badlands . . . it is not clear why there is such a hurry to open part of the reservation unless it is entirely in the interest of some railroad or a few settlers along the north part of the reserve.[4]

He assessed that area to be "better than any other portion of the reservation at the present time [because] the majority of the people living on the strip are mixed bloods and are fairly industrious and self supporting, are allotted and are in possession of their trust patents." However, Brennan was forced to conclude that, despite their industriousness, many were not ready for citizenship.

Against Brennan's better judgment, on September 1, 1909, a meeting was held concerning the opening of the reservation to non-Indian settlement. Brennan's opening remarks included an ominous message about the importance of this meeting: "[It] will probably mean the beginning of the opening of a portion of your reservation to white settlers and the beginning of the breaking up of your tribal relations."[5] Fullbloods evaded the question of opening any part of their reservation to non-Indians, demanding a reconsideration of what they considered to be extreme abuses of the Treaty of 1868. They did not see how it would be possible for them to discuss the relinquishment of more land when the previous treaty had been so egregiously broken.

Unfortunately, in 1903, another "white man's law," *Lone Wolf v Hitchcock* (Prucha 1990:202–3) gave the federal government the right to abrogate treaties made with Indians, as long as it was acting in "the utmost good faith" as their guardians (Harring 1994:147). As described in the council meeting of September 9, 1909, the substance of the *Lone Wolf* decision was that "the Government was the guardian of the Indians; that guardians have the right to do that which is deemed best for their wards and that Congress has the power vested in it to open Indian reservations without obtaining the consent of the Indians thereto."[6] Indeed, *Lone Wolf* further defined and expanded Congress's plenary power over Indians, and has been referred to as the "Indians' Dred Scott decision" (Hanson 1980:459–84).

One fullblood representative from the Wakpamni district of Pine Ridge saw things very differently with respect to the issue of guardianship:

> And you [Brennan and Major James McLaughlin] also said something that is laughable, that congressmen were the guardians of the Indians and they could do just as they saw fit. I think you made a mistake on that, I think we are the guardians of the white people instead of them being the guardians of us, because we have been giving them land ever since they crossed the ocean up to the present day.[7]

The council was primarily attended by fullbloods who were not in favor of the opening; mixedbloods, if in attendance, did not take the floor, or at least are not mentioned in the official report of the meeting. McLaughlin extended the opportunity to discuss the matter further after dinner, but most decided that they had said all that they had to say and opted to consider the meeting concluded. The following day, however, some unnamed mixedbloods spoke with McLaughlin about changing some of the borders of the proposed opening, indicating that they, and perhaps some of the fullbloods, had rethought their options. They suggested another meeting in a town within the area to be opened, perhaps thinking that a group including more mixedbloods might be more amenable to change.

This political strategy was a distinct break from the traditional manner of dealing with the federal government. It was more common for the older men who comprised the chiefs' council to speak for the tribe. Harry Anderson, an historian of South Dakota who has studied the increasing political role of mixedbloods on Rosebud Reservation, argued, with respect to a similar 1889 meeting, that "this open rebellion by the younger whites and mixed bloods against the authority of the chiefs would not have been tolerated a decade before . . . Although it is difficult to follow the trend down to the present day, this seems to have been the beginning of the development of the mixed-blooded population as a major influence in the political life of the Rosebud Sioux" (Anderson 1973:269). The same appears to have been the case on Pine Ridge Reservation as well.

One mixedblood, speaking for other mixedbloods during the hearings regarding the ceding of land on Rosebud Reservation, which borders Bennett County on the east, argued that "every man is supposed to have his own opinion in regard to this business. It is not left with a body of men [meaning the chiefs' council] to decide upon this matter" (Anderson 1973:268). It would appear that Valentine T. McGillicuddy, agent at Pine Ridge some twenty years before, had succeeded in getting his message across. He subscribed to the "every man his own chief" theory in encouraging individualism and insisted that the system allowing chiefs to enhance their prestige by redistributing annuities to their bands should give way to one in which heads of households would receive their own directly. As a result, "when [McGillicuddy] arrived in 1879 there were eleven bands with as many chiefs; a year later the number had increased to thirty" (DeMallie 1978:253). Another historian of the Sioux noted that by 1881 there were sixty-three chiefs requesting rations for their families (Utley 1963:28).

As requested, a second council was held on September 15, 1909 in Allen, which lay in the northwestern corner of the Pass Creek district of Pine Ridge that was slated for opening. Of the eighty Lakotas present, only Charles Turning Hawk, Bull Bear, Horn Cloud, Good Lance, Lone Hill, Plenty Bear, and Long Commander rose to speak their opinions. They were clearly the representatives of the chiefs' council and put forth the standard fullblood positions on the matter. Despite McLaughlin's attempts to appeal to individuals by noting in his opening remarks, "I have not yet been in an assembly of this size that found every person of one mind,"[8] the chiefs' council still held sway, even in this district where a large proportion of mixedbloods resided, despite the revision of history presented in the official Bennett County history.[9]

Turning Hawk argued that allotment of land to Indians had not been completed, and that the government should wait for a couple of years before opening the county, to allow Lakotas to develop a better understanding of the bill's implications. The minutes of the September 9, 1909 meeting in Pine Ridge stated that it had taken McLaughlin "one hour and a quarter" to read the bill in council.[10] It should be remembered that most Lakota fullbloods were not literate at that time, and that even if they had been, it would be difficult to fully assess the legal complexities of such a document after one reading, so Turning Hawk's appeal was well reasoned. He closed his remarks with an apt analogy of the persistent and impatient government commissioners who were not allowing Lakotas to digest the full implications of the bill. "Uncle Sam is like the coyote who took the carcass to the water to make it soft. He returned to the carcass often to see if it had softened in the water. We do not think we are soft yet." Bull Bear worried that "we don't know how much of this land is surplus land.

I do not think you know either. I do not think you know how many people are not allotted."[11] Horn Cloud's comments reflect the lack of real interaction between the fullbloods and others in the district, except when it was expedient for the mixedbloods and whites: "The white men living on the reservation and the mixed bloods, never advise us in any way but now when this thing comes up they tell us it is good for us and it surprised us. If they showed us something like this [the proposed bill] before we would understand and would be willing to take their advice now."[12]

The themes of treaty violations and governmental impatience ran through each response from the representatives of the chiefs' council. Plenty Bear's discourse summed up their feelings eloquently:

> My friend, I tell you to take my words home and tell them to the President and his men. We are going to fill the land so do not bother us now because the people are allotting yet. If you wait until we are through allotting and there is a half a foot left, the Oglalas will say so. You owe us much by the treaties you make with us and give us only a little part of it. We have only a small piece left. That is the reason I'm very much afraid of the President. We wanted to be so good that we are having a hard time. When they are through allotting, what is left we want to go in this way. When you ask for such a great big piece you surprise us. Now you cannot say that this certain piece of land named in the bill will come to much money. We Indians here do not understand anything like that. Then when we get so we understand more and we see that it does not benefit us we tell you.[13]

After listening to the seven representatives, McLauglin closed the meeting by explaining certain provisions of the bill with the ominous message that "no matter what the decision of the Oglala Council maybe [sic], there is a possibility of the land being thrown open anyhow."[14]

Summing up the two councils' implications for the opening of Bennett County, it did not really matter much whether or not the Lakotas agreed. *Lone Wolf* upheld the government's power to abrogate treaties unilaterally, so the decision could be implemented over the complaints of Lakotas. By proposing the opening in council, the government postured an earnest concern for their dependent wards, while fullbloods and mixedbloods became further divided. Fullbloods continued to argue for rights guaranteed by treaty, as well as the return of the Black Hills; mixedbloods attempted coalitions and conciliation that might increase their prestige and power with the United States government. The tension between resistance to and collusion with imposed federal policies caused a rift that still remains in Bennett County and on Pine Ridge Reservation.

The following year, not unexpectedly, the South Dakota legislature opened Bennett County, distinguishing it from Pine Ridge Reservation and further diminishing reservation land by 1,173 square miles.[15] For administrative purposes, however, Bennett County was still attached to Fall River County, which administered the area of Pine Ridge Reservation, levying and collecting taxes. Naturally, from the very outset, residents of Bennett County began discussing the feasibility of petitioning the governor for full autonomy, fearing that they would be responsible for paying taxes without receiving their fair share of benefits from Fall River.

With one foot in each culture, mixedbloods found a new role as cultural elite. They were able to proclaim their "competency" by virtue of owning taxable land, and thereby achieve the status of United States citizens. It should be noted that it was not until later, in 1924, that all Indians were granted U.S. citizenship through the Indian Citizenship Act (Prucha 1990:218; see discussion in Prucha 1984, 2:793–94). Many were also able to gain the support of fullbloods through their connections to their *thiyóšpaye*. Although many mixedbloods had severed their tribal ties, their *thiyóšpaye* did not necessarily sever its ties to them, and they were able to garner some measure of political power by drawing support from a diversity of groups in certain short-term situations. Ultimately, however, they were marginalized by both whites and fullbloods. Whites still perceived them as inferior, "on the road to civilization" but far from arriving. Fullbloods increasingly perceived them as traitors, and in no way valued their "achievements" as a new class of "red whitemen," this very term attesting to the Lakota perception of "white" as a cultural category rather than a racial one. Fullbloods attempted to exclude mixedbloods when filing lawsuits against the federal government for the illegal taking of the Black Hills because they were seen as having given up their Lakota birthright early on (see Lazarus 1991).

One such mixedblood was Henry Cottier, who in his eighties, proclaimed "I am an Indian. I am glad and proud of it. All that I am and all that I have, I am and I have because I am an Indian. Perhaps the only time I ever wished I wasn't quite so much Indian – notice I said, 'Quite so much Indian' – was when my future father-in-law was giving my future wife hell because she wanted to marry me, and I had a few more drops of Indian blood in my veins than she had" (Lewis 1980:199).[16] Cottier went on to offer a theory about his distant relative, Crazy Horse, a powerful symbol of Lakota identity because of his leading role at the Battle of the Little Bighorn and his unflagging resistance to Lakota confinement on reservations: "From what my parents told me of him, there is little doubt in my mind that he is part white like my mother. He had light brown, almost blonde hair, and his eyes were not black like the Indians, but a curious kind of brown with lighter flecks. Neither was his skin of the same color and texture as the skin of the other Indians" (Lewis 1980:201). It was the custom to give early names to Lakota children who had not yet distinguished themselves in battle or otherwise. Those familiar names were often based upon a physical or behavioral characteristic, and Crazy Horse's childhood names were Curly, and sometimes, Light-Haired Boy. It is interesting to note that there are no known photographs of Crazy Horse. Because of this ambiguity, Crazy Horse is a powerful and multivalent symbol for Lakotas – for fullbloods because of his indefatigable resistance to the encroaching white settlers and military, and for mixedbloods because of the possibility that he had non-Indian ancestors (for an account of this, see Ambrose 1975:38). Cottier, while proud of being "Indian," was also proud to cast one of the most prestigious leaders of the Lakotas as a mixedblood.

As a non-Indian married to a Lakota woman and adoptee into the tribe, Henry Cottier's father had been eligible for an allotment under the terms of the 1868 treaty. Cottier grew to understand western concepts of private property, land allotment, and the counting and categorizing of people by race by virtue of his job as allotment agent and, later, as taker of the 1910 census for the South Dakota Indian population. He was typical of mixedbloods of that time who, though having only minimal education, were hired to work for the Indian Service.

After Bennett County was opened in 1910, Cottier realized that unless it was formally organized before all the non-Indian newcomers came to claim their land, power in the new county would pass entirely into non-Indian hands. Frustrated by the attempts of a few non-Indian men to hold up the official organization of the county until incoming non-Indians had taken possession of their parcels of land, he took the initiative to collect the necessary signatures from county residents, and hand-delivered them to the governor (*Bennett County Booster I,* Feb. 28, 1912:1; Jan. 17, 1912:1). He did this despite valid fullblood protests that not all Indians had received their allotments, and despite their fear that the best land would be given to non-Indian settlers. The local newspaper editor, a staunch supporter of independent county organization, reported that "many of the mixedbloods are more progressive than a majority of white men in pioneer communities and are counted well-to-do men. It augers well for the new county if they must 'take up the white man's burden' of a new form of government" (*Bennett County Booster I,* Feb. 28, 1912:1). With all the talk of "progressive" mixedbloods, fullbloods became further marginalized as residents continued to internalize the distinction between fullbloods and mixedbloods in terms of competency and citizenship. Failing to mention that his own non-Indian father had married into the tribe and was one of the white men allotted land, Cottier leveled accusations against others in the same circumstance who were attempting to hold up county organization.

Cottier must have realized that an early organization of the county would assure him a position of power, since he had held responsible jobs in the non-Indian world and was able to gain the support of many other mixed-bloods. Once the county was settled by non-Indians, mixedbloods would become an even more vulnerable minority, but in the meantime, non-Indians depended on mixedblood support for formal organization, which would allow them to stake their own claims to primacy and power before the new settlers arrived. Cottier's faction succeeded in pushing the organization through, and on April 9, 1912 the county held its first elections, choosing officers whose terms would last only until January 1, 1913. While at first the vast majority of officers were mixedbloods, in the election held the following year, many of those were replaced, and by World War I, mixedbloods were, for the most part, out of power (see Bennett County Historical Society 1981:6–7; *Bennett County Booster I,* April 10, 1912:1; also January 17, 1912:1).

Thus, from the very inception of Bennett County, land tenure has been a major factor in shaping social identity. Early non-Indian settlers attempting to secede from Pine Ridge Reservation argued that, by holding deeded (taxable) rather than allotted (nontaxable) land, mixedbloods would be able to free themselves from the "tyranny" of fullbloods, who controlled reservation politics by privileging members of their own *thiyóšpaye,* and obtain "real" power by holding county offices. The only Indians qualified to vote in the election to secede from the reservation were mixedbloods and a few fullbloods who held their land in deeded status; other Lakotas were not able to vote without relinquishing their relationship to the tribe and converting their land to taxable status. Those mixedbloods who did just that were accused by fullbloods of selling out their Lakota birthright and tribal land base.

It is easy to understand that, given the contested nature of the original settlement and opening of the county, old grudges find expression from time to time, in unexpected places. The sites of contestation are often ones that involve issues of territory and identity and are often highlighted by issues of contest in larger social fields, such as in national debates on race, ethnicity, and personal identity. In this case, the national issue of negative portrayals of ethnic identity in Indian mascots brought relevant issues in a local community sharply into focus.

CONTEXTUALIZING THE HOMECOMING SNAPSHOTS

Here we have the opportunity to widen the initial view of homecoming weekend by considering it in the context of Bennett County history, adding substance to the previous description of events. The analysis from this angle will add depth that outsiders may not have perceived on their first viewing of the narrative snapshots.

Edward Spicer (1971) identified a condition that operates in intercultural relations and leads to the reinforcement of what he refers to as "persistent cultural systems." In this, "cultural blindness" on the part of a dominant society opens a space that allows subordinated cultural entities to endure and strengthen (Spicer 1994). While the gazes of those in power are averted, marginalized groups continue life as usual, but with heightened feelings of difference and otherness because they have, once again, been rendered invisible. This condition was evidenced in Martin when local people chose to view the Thursday afternoon march from behind their curtains. By not attending the rally that followed, they could maintain their points of view without hearing the demonstrators' complaints and then considering whether or not those were valid. As a result, the marchers came away with their feelings of marginalization validated. They could continue to view the local community as racist, and would then redouble their efforts to disrupt the homecoming ceremony later that night. They needed to feel that they were seen, at the very least, as human beings, some of whom lived in the community, with grievances that were worthy of addressing.

When reconsidering the homecoming ceremony itself, it seems obvious that county residents and demonstrators interpreted this secular ritual through differing worldviews. Perceiving the situation primarily in terms of race and phenotype, some white and mixedblood county residents were secure in the fact that they were an inclusive non-racist community. After all, the royalty were "Indians." But more precisely, in the reality of the social field that is Bennett County, and in the language of existing social categories, they were mixedbloods whose families were relatively successful as ranchers and farmers and who did not as a rule maintain proper kinship relations with fullblood relatives. The social division between them had happened over the years, beginning with early political alliances between mixedbloods and whites at the expense of fullbloods. Conversely, fullblood "outsiders" (including some fullbloods who were otherwise local "insiders" by virtue of living in the county) identified those same mixedbloods as culturally non-Indian in terms of their value systems and class. While the homecoming royalty were from racially mixed backgrounds, they were light years away from living a traditional kinship-based Lakota way of life. Closer analysis suggests that, in this case, non-Indian and mixedblood residents understood identity in terms of degree of Indian blood – racially – while fullblood Lakotas viewed identity in terms of an historically and socially based ethnicity requiring maintenance of proper relational values and obligations. The difference between Lakota and distinctly individualistic values will be discussed at some length in chapter 3.

In direct counterpoint to the protest march, in which demonstrators were rendered, for all intents and purposes, invisible, the homecoming parade enjoyed visibility. This was an idealized tableau of a community that got along and was able to embrace and applaud difference, reinforcing the community ideal of equality, civility, and friendship. This melting pot ideal was reflected in the well-scrubbed faces of fullblood, mixedblood, and white students riding on colorful floats and waving exuberantly to their relatives lining Main Street. No one viewed this event from behind curtains. The only people remaining inside the stores were those few souls unlucky enough to be selling camera film and other conveniences to those of us who took rolls and rolls of photos or ran out of smokes, but even they had a great view through their sparkling storefront windows. The community's reflection of itself was framed in a mirror of cooperation and participation. *E pluribus unum* at last – Indian and white together in accord, the way it always "was"; the way it always "should be." But must a mirror necessarily reflect the same image to everyone involved?

Barbara Myerhoff and Stephen Mongulla's (1986) analysis of a solidarity walk organized by members of the Los Angeles Jewish community stresses the importance of understanding historical contexts when considering events that link diverse groups. Their study examined what divided Jews in Los Angeles into subgroups labeled Orthodox, Reform, Conservative, affiliated, nonaffiliated, Hasidic, Sephardic, Ashkenazic, or Yordic. A "common sense" of Jewishness still admitted internal boundaries that highlighted differences in interpretation of what makes a human being a Jew. More specifically, here it was ideas regarding proper ways of living that distinguished one group of Jews from another. The organizers of the Los Angeles solidarity walk needed to deal with each group as a discrete entity, yet success would only be achieved if a true sense of unity could be created out of the welter of diversity. Here, as in Bennett County, for those internal differences to be overcome, larger and smaller social fields had to be addressed and then brought into harmony. This required finding a common field of social experience, and that field was what distinguished Jews from non-Jews – not unlike the county pride encouraged by the organizers of the Bennett County homecoming parade.

Myerhoff and Mongulla (1986:120) analyzed the event through two modes of understanding, first "as the product of the historical situation," and second "as an improvisation in uncertainty." The former "suggests lines of interpretation and offers 'appropriate' symbols"; the latter requires the participants to play their expected roles, while at the same time allowing for the possibility that "their performance is not doing what they want it to do." The problem of selecting and mobilizing appropriate symbols to be invested with meaning is no easy task, especially when groups lack the cohesion of one common worldview and share a regional history of subordination, as in Bennett County.

The Warrior symbolism was appropriate at the time of its adoption over sixty years before, intended to capture the experience of men and women who, whether fullblood, mixedblood, or white, had served their country in The Great War. At the time, two of the high school coaches were Indian men; one from Wisconsin who lived at Rosebud Reservation, and the other a local Dakota Episcopalian minister. They did not object, and the Warrior symbolism remained unproblematic for years. One non-Indian Warrior Princess from the 1950s recalled what an exciting experience it had been to be a candidate. She said that it had been a great educational experience to visit the Pine Ridge family who would loan her their Indian clothing and accessories to wear and to listen intently and respectfully as family members explained how the clothing had been made, each beaded or feathered object having a special significance, often related in stories. She said that she recalled those stories as she processed up the aisle at homecoming, and that she wore the clothing with great care. In another conversation, she told me that the practice was discontinued several years later, when it was claimed that one piece of regalia had not been returned to its rightful owner. She did not know whether that was true, noting that if it was true, it was a wrong thing to do. Beyond such personal reminiscences, events and issues at the national level in 1996 affected how the Warrior symbol was viewed, with a negative effect on the community. Perhaps the institution of another symbol was in order.

Precedents for this exist; many schools, such as Juniata College, where I am now employed, have changed their names and logos to accommodate Indian wishes – but never unproblematically. Some Juniata alumni, themselves members and supporters of previous Juniata teams, threatened to withdraw monetary support to the alumni fund if such a change occurred. However, Indian activist, actor, and author Russell Means, a Lakota who is himself a mixedblood descendant of Major Charles Allen (a non-Indian for whom an unincorporated town in Bennett County was named, and a significant force in South Dakota history) prevailed in his pleas, and the school dropped the name "Juniata Indians." We are now the Eagles. One alumnus saved the day when he designed and proposed a logo depicting a highly stylized eagle in flight, wings caught on the down stroke. It was an ambiguous and multivalent symbol that looks both like an eagle in flight and a feathered Plains Indian headdress. This was an acceptable change for a Pennsylvania college, despite the fact that Plains-style feathered war bonnets were never worn by the Susquehannocks and Lenni Lenapes who had lived in the area. But Juniata does not have the same historical context, and is not situated between the Pine Ridge and Rosebud reservations. Different contexts call for different solutions.

The Bennett County homecoming parade succeeded in presenting a positive self-image that the community needed to see. But on another level, the homecoming weekend in general was a failure for all involved because it once again brought contested spaces and identities into clear view, both locally and nationally. The circumstances surrounding this homecoming ceremony – a product of Bennett County's historical situation that suddenly took center stage in a national political debate – do not suggest an "appropriate" symbol that might unify the diverse regional population. No one is willing to lose another inch of territory, be it in terms of identity, land, or symbols, especially when the whole world is watching.

The case of the Juniata College "Indian" team name and logo illustrates issues of ethnic identity. According to Anya Peterson Royce (1982), ethnic identity is doubly bounded and is viewed (and assigned) through the different perspectives of "insider" and "outsider," each with its own standard for judging a social actor's performance of ethnicity. For residents of Pennsylvania who have stereotypical notions of "Indian" because they know rural Indian people only through the representations of Indianness in popular culture (themselves stereotypical), strong arguments can be made for abandoning stereotypical representations; for instance, mascots and logos. The representation of Indianness that still appears in tiles above the front door of the college library is of a Plains Indian, not depicted in garb worn by historical Pennsylvania Indian groups. The Juniata image was a stereotypical one, drawing upon an idea of the Plains Indian as the "authentic" Indian, and when Means came to object, it was arguably appropriate to make changes.

However, in Bennett County, the Warrior symbol was instituted by Indian football coaches as a logo that represented those who fought in the World Wars – Indian and non-Indian alike. In that historical time and space, the underlying symbolism was of Bennett County as a region of diverse neighbors. Since a fuller understanding of what constitutes Indianness applied, stereotypical representations performed by demonstrators did not have the power that they do in other places. Also, in that social context, many fullbloods identified strongly with their sense of being graduates or students of Bennett County High School, not primarily with their identities as fullblood Lakotas. One related to me that the school had provided opportunities for his family, each of whom had completed his or her studies and then enrolled at Oglala Lakota College or elsewhere. He found the demonstration unwarranted and embarrassing. He went on to note, however, that he was irate about the mascot of the Cleveland Indians, named "Chief Yahoo," and the "tomahawk chop" of the Atlanta Braves. He believed that those teams and their fans did not understand Indians or their cultures, and that those symbols promoted racist and stereotypical images of American Indians. He, like many other fullbloods, believes that the mascot issue detracts attention from more important issues faced by American Indian peoples, such as treaty rights and questions of sovereignty.

THREE

Social Selves

There is, even where the sense of place is embittered, conflictual, sorrowing, or . . . a bit worked up, or even where things seem to be, as they seem to be everywhere, fragile, abrading, or sliding away, a pervading air of "we belong here" intimacy. GEERTZ 1996:260

This chapter considers the social fields internal to Bennett County, especially in relation to land and kinship. Before offering narrative snapshots of a tragic event that occurred six months into my fieldwork, some foundation concerning social identities will be laid, this time considering differing worldviews of the three local social categories, fullblood, mixedblood, and white. It must be stressed that even in contemporary life, certain of the historical cultural and phenotypic generalizations that led to these categories are very apparent, and very real. Differences may be highlighted, from time to time, as during the homecoming protest and the homecoming ceremony, or they may be bridged, as in the homecoming parade. Even in times of relative community stasis, old historical grievances wait just below the surface, and when they emerge, especially in community crises, they are expressed in racial terms. Particularly in a small community, such crises can be devastating, their effects passed down from generation to generation.

Coming from the Chicago area, I understand racial and ethnic politics as complicated. From my urban perspective, I was surprised to find precious little diversity in Bennett County beyond Indian, white, and variations on those themes. Many of the local residents are descendants of people listed on original reservation allotment rolls and in early county records; those residents are considered insiders in the regional social field. Outsiders who marry into well-established non-Indian regional families are considered to be valuable members of their community – most of the time. In times of severe community stress, however, they are reminded, in no uncertain terms and as a matter of social fact, that their opinions may not carry as much weight as the opinions of insiders born in the county (see, for example, Elias and Scotson 1994; Martindale and Hanson 1971; Baumgartner 1988).

CONTEMPORARY BENNETT COUNTY

Bennett County is an expanse of rolling prairie comprising approximately 1,173 square miles that at the time of this study supported a population of 3,206, of whom 1,151 resided in Martin, the county seat and only formally organized town. Averaging approximately three per square mile, residents of Bennett County boast about "breathing room," but there is little boasting about the economy, which has always been weak. This rural area is kept afloat primarily by family operated farms and cattle ranches, many of those helped in turn by federal aid to farmers and ranchers, general assistance, and BIA programs for the Indian community. Recent federal budgetary constraints have heightened tensions between neighbors vying for limited funds. In addition, environmental, cultural, and demographic factors divide South Dakota into "East River" and "West River" regions along the one-hundredth meridian (see map 1). East of the Missouri River lie rich farm lands and larger urban centers with a population that considers itself to be much more cosmopolitan. By comparison, West River people, in general, are marginalized. Farms and ranches, no matter how large, are limited in production capacity by land characteristics and climate, and the state tourism industry's attempt to capitalize on the "Wild West" character of the area does not yet yield substantial income. Towns are farther apart in West River and, consequently, highway construction and road maintenance are of prime concern to locals who must transport their goods to distant processing centers. While a guest and featured speaker of the local Commercial Club, Governor William Janklow of South Dakota reminded the mayor of Martin, who had been arguing politely for the allocation of more state highway funds for this county, about the "golden rule": "Those who've got the gold, *rule!*" Thus, this geographically and economically challenged county is also underprivileged in state politics.

The major contemporary economic problem in Bennett County, a shrinking tax base coupled with escalating demands for city and county services, is made more acute by multiple types of land tenure (see map 2). Legal relationships to land became particularly problematic and relevant to discussion of local social categories when racialized land policies opened new fiscal opportunities for certain members of the population. The greater part of the land (535,370 of the county's 762,798 acres categorized as agricultural land, in addition to approximately 11,000 acres of non-agricultural platted land in the Martin city limits and roadways) is held in deeded taxable status.[1] For the most part, it is this taxable land base that finances vital county services, including education, law enforcement, fire control, and road maintenance.

Approximately 192,258 acres of nontaxable land is currently held in trust for the Oglala Sioux Tribe or individual tribal members by the federal government, which allocates funds to defray the costs of public education for Indian children whose families do not pay county taxes. This aid is a provision of the Johnson-O'Malley Act, passed in 1934, in keeping with the federal government's desire for a New Deal for Indians in the form of the Indian Reorganization Act,[2] intended to increase Indian self-determination (Prucha 1990:221–22). The federal contribution generally amounts to approximately one-third of the actual tax value, not fully compensating for lost county revenue.

The Lacreek National Wildlife Refuge, administered by the U.S. Fish and Wildlife Service, occupies 16,400 acres of nontaxable federal land. A large portion of the refuge was removed from the county tax base in 1935, when, by eminent domain, it was taken from Indian allottees and non-Indian taxpayers alike. One non-Indian woman who lived through the ordeal related the story of her mother collecting a minuscule sum of money for her property, then watching while bulldozers razed their small log cabin. She recalled an idyllic life on the wetlands, where the soil is richer than in any other location in the county, and noted that her mother never recovered emotionally from the loss. My friend expressed her family's newly realized sense of marginalization by saying, "They treated us just like Indians. They just came and pushed us off our land." Later, the government bought out a large cattle ranch to add to the refuge acreage, removing it from the tax base as well. Federal monies, again amounting to approximately one-third of the actual tax value, are paid to the county in compensation for lost tax revenue, but the human tragedy cannot be addressed in monetary terms alone.

Land and loss became common themes in my interviews with oldtimers, and resentment became an even more common theme when I spoke with their children. A longstanding dispute between the federal government and the owners of land surrounding the refuge concerns certain refuge policies, particularly water and drainage policies that have led to reduced productivity at nearby ranches, and the reluctance on the part of the refuge to reduce the spread of Canadian thistle. Landowners basically have been told that the court case could drag on for years, and that the government had unlimited funds for attorneys. I attended a meeting, held in a meeting room at the rural cooperative electric company, between the landowners and federal representatives. Much of what I observed paralleled accounts of meetings between Indians and federal officials concerning the opening of Bennett County. Federal representatives postured concern, but I still came away with the feeling that the government was simply

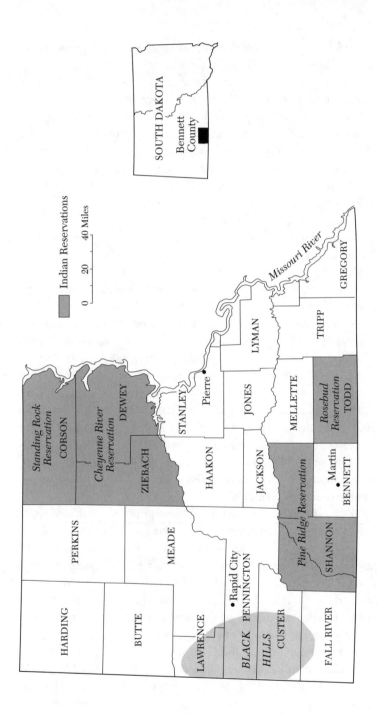

1. West River Country of South Dakota

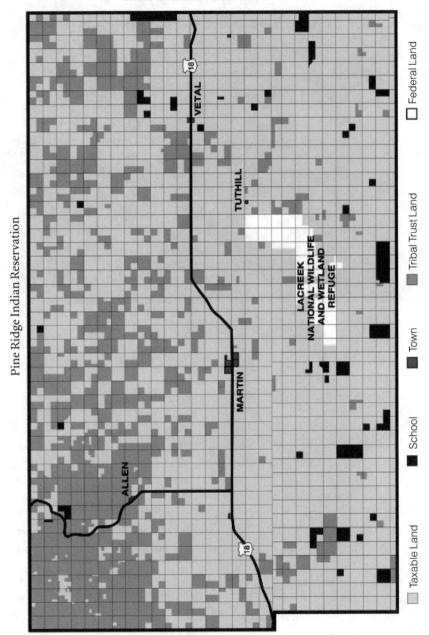

Rosebud Indian Reservation

Pine Ridge Indian Reservation

Pine Ridge Indian Reservation

VETAL

TUTHILL

MARTIN

ALLEN

LACREEK
NATIONAL WILDLIFE
AND WETLAND
REFUGE

Federal Land

Tribal Trust Land

Town

School

Taxable Land

2. Bennett County, South Dakota

13. Lacreek National Wildlife and Wetland Refuge

humoring the landowners in the same way that they humored Lakotas some eighty-five years before.

In addition to coping with problems brought on by the Lacreek refuge, many who still live near the refuge must cope with enormous flocks of migrating geese, as well as geese that have become virtually domesticated over the years, bold enough to eat newly sewn seeds out of the ground right in front of a landowner. One resourceful non-Indian landowner simply set up a bird hunting enterprise. Hunters armed with shotguns line his ditches every fall, dressed in khaki, faces smeared with camouflage paint, waiting for one of the unsuspecting birds to fly over the fence onto private land so that it could become a trophy, a dinner, or both. The first time that I saw twenty commandos scrunched down in the trenches, I was both awed and terribly afraid. I had hoped that I was not the enemy.

Finally, scattered throughout the county are 17,470 acres of state lands set aside as school sections. While the state pays no taxes on these lands, certain vacant parcels are leased as grazing land. In such cases, the lessee is required to pay county tax.

This complex arrangement effectively splits the county into taxpayer and non-taxpayer factions. In political discussions about the wildlife refuge, that split is often couched in anti-federal-government rhetoric. However, in conversations about taxes, the division is generally expressed in terms of race, with allusions to the competency of taxpayers, the incompetency of Indians living on nontaxable allotments or tribal trust land, and the strategizing of mixedbloods who claim Indian status to avoid paying taxes. A few of the non-Indian residents place the responsibility for such racial tension directly on the federal government, but most residents do not, at least not explicitly, make that connection.

How did issues of land tenure, race, competency, and incompetency become so inextricably entwined in Bennett County? To answer this question it is necessary first to discuss what the local social categories of identity are, how land came to be seen as a commodity, and how Indian blood quantum ratios came to be used as indices of legal identity. Juxtaposing Euro-American cultural notions of proper relationships to land and kin and those of the Lakotas and exploring how they both have changed over time exposes differences in how people classify their worlds and how the "other" is constructed and perceived in the regional social field.

THREE SOCIAL CATEGORIES

Who are fullbloods, mixedbloods, and whites in Bennett County? The groups may be distinguished from one another phenotypically, of course, in terms of characteristics arranged along a somewhat arbitrary continuum of human physical characteristics. However, as those social categories are understood in everyday interactions, they also have nonracial connotations. Factors such as whether county residents hold their land in deeded or allotted status, whether they live in town or out in the country, in Indian "cluster housing" or on their allotments, and whether they are "educated" or still speak Lakota as their first language become important indicators of externally and internally perceived identities. Of course, those identities, once named, acquire more rigid boundaries and definitions. It should go without saying that in real life, all identities are contingent upon their social, legal, and historical contexts. No categorizations of human beings fit perfectly at all times, in all social, historical, or legal contexts, and the boundaries between people are always constructed out of so-called social facts and realities (see, for example, Moore 1986).

Fullbloods

The prototypical fullblood is a traditional Lakota. Fullbloods pride themselves on the fact that their ancestors fought against outside forces pressuring them to assimilate into the dominant culture and continued holding their treaty rights sacrosanct. Family histories are passed down through the generations, highlighting their connections to ancestors who rode with Crazy Horse and Red Cloud against the U.S. Cavalry. They perceive themselves as a nation, both in terms of internal social connections and because they were recognized as such by authorized representatives of the United States who signed treaties with the various bands of Sioux. Proficiency in the "old" Lakota language is also a requirement for being recognized as a "real" fullblood by other fullbloods. Cultural continuity may be surmised when one's elders pass down the Lakota language to younger family members as their primary language, with English being the second language learned in school. However, not many Lakota families are able to continue in the old language, given the pervasiveness of English in schools, the economic sphere, and the media. There are several ongoing attempts to intensively reinvigorate the language at the *thiyóšpaye* level.

Robert Daniels (1970) collected a list of stereotypical assumptions about fullbloods, all of which stem from misunderstandings of cultural difference. Many stereotypes portrayed fullbloods in terms of incompetence, as people lacking in industry and "good sense." Given differences in the American and Lakota kinship systems, as well as significant differences in the two cultures' view of one's relationship to land, it is not difficult to trace the roots of contemporary racism to language concerning the dependence, wardship, and incompetency of Indians in federal Indian policies. Such attitudes have been passed down unselfconsciously through the generations and, in some cases, internalized. According to Daniels, many whites, and many of the more assimilated mixedbloods who had, from time to time, referred to fullbloods as "blanket Indians," believe that

> full-bloods live in poverty because they don't care, are slow-witted, waste their money on alcohol and no-good relatives, and waste their time on dances and tooling around the countryside in cars they don't maintain . . . have no respect for personal property, either their own or other people's . . . are unreliable employees because they are always late (on "Indian time"), are lazy, and can only be given limited responsibilities . . . prefer to make a living, miserable as it is, by deception, by sexual immorality (through Aid to Dependent Children welfare checks), and by seeking federal and tribal handouts rather than holding down an honest job or putting their land to use . . . spoil their children with candy and with toys that are soon broken and neglected, but they don't care enough to see that the children are properly fed or get a proper education. Full-blooded children go undisciplined. [Daniels 1970:208]

During my stay in Bennett County, twenty-five years after Daniels's, I found that those attitudes had not changed significantly. Stereotypical perceptions of fullbloods remain based on values that underlay early non-Indian misunderstandings of cultural difference. Non-Indians and upwardly mobile mixedbloods often describe fullbloods with the rhetoric of incompetence, annuity payments, and a general lack of interest in "proper" education.[3] In many ways, these stereotypes are analogous to those applied to marginalized minorities in other social contexts and therefore may be understood as socially structured and nested hierarchical forms awaiting content.

On the other hand, fullbloods are, at other times, viewed positively by some of the more conservative non-Indians, who compare them favorably to mixedbloods as people strong enough to maintain their traditions. Many non-Indians are proud of their families' long term relationships with Lakota families, perhaps their neighbors in "the old days." Non-Indian oldtimers recall times when they got stuck at a Lakota friend's home and had to wait for snow or rainstorms to blow over, passing the time by telling stories, playing cards, or just gossiping. Sometimes they would have to avail themselves of Indian hospitality for a week or more, and they gladly returned the favor when their friends were in need. The plains weather built bonds between people who recognized that human beings could die in sudden storms, and the weather highlighted a common humanity rather than its divisions. One non-Indian community leader expressed it this way: "In the old days we were all the same out here. We were all poor." Another non-Indian rancher and political leader informed me, directly and in no uncertain terms, that he would have to check me out before he would introduce me to any of his Indian friends who live on their allotments in the country near Allen. He said that he "would rather take a bullet [in his own] head" than introduce his Indian friends to an anthropologist before finding out what her intentions were.

I learned that while the bonds between oldtimers were strong, sometimes relations between their children were not. One informant broke into reluctant tears as she related a story about the time that she was accused of being a racist by the son of her dear friend and longtime neighbor, who was a fullblood. She traces the problem today to fullblood kids who have gone off to college in the cities and come back with "hateful" ideas. When pressed, she described those hateful ideas as an all-consuming materialism and legal savvy. She said that nowadays, young Indian neighbors are more interested in maintaining their physical and metaphorical fences than in actively neighboring.

Whatever the reason, most residents agree that race relations were better in the "old days," at least in the days before the termination era of the 1950s, when many Indian people were encouraged (and on some reservations, forced) to relocate to large urban centers to find work (see Deloria 1944; Nagel 1997; Means and Wolf 1995; and Prucha 1990, 1984). After some bitter experiences in urban ghettos, the only housing option available for people forced to look for work that they were unprepared to accomplish, they reconsidered their options (see Deloria 1944). Missing their relatives and the social support that they provided, they returned home, bringing back urban ideas that could not be reconciled with the tenuously negotiated social equilibrium. Some local educators dealing with the devastating effects of a second generation of fetal alcohol syndrome attribute it to the urban experience, where Lakota women were introduced to the practice of drinking in bars.

The city in the 1950s was a difficult place for fullbloods who did not already have family there. Many of those who persisted were, in the end, successful. Some who made a life for themselves there returned home frequently, and networks were formed for other family members seeking to come to the cities for temporary work or urban schooling. The result is that contemporary Lakotas are able to move back and forth between social networks that have been built over the years.

Whether or not problems between neighbors in Bennett County are a direct result of fullbloods being "contaminated" by outside forces is basically an issue of perception. In any case, that perception is held by many local oldtimers – fullblood, mixedblood, and non-Indians alike.

Mixedbloods

The Treaty of 1868 was one of the most important historical events for the Lakotas, as well as for white men who had married Lakota women and mixedbloods. The treaty created the Great Sioux Reservation, firmly established the agency system, and provided the white husbands of Indian women, and their offspring, legal status as tribal members (Anderson 1973:245). Mixedbloods became "a progressive force that repeatedly sought, or supported, the implementation of new government policies for the Sioux. Often their motivation was highly personal," and they saw those policies as "a means for self-improvement as well as an inevitable encroachment of the whites upon the Sioux way of life that could not be successfully resisted" (Anderson 1973:269). They also were quick to claim their allotments, while the fullbloods, who actively resisted federal policies through their non-participation in government schemes, chose to be assigned allotments by a federal agent after four years. By then, the more productive agricultural land had been allotted to more enthusiastic participants who were, for the most part, either mixedbloods or white heads of households.

Mixedbloods are generally thought of, both by local fullbloods and by whites, as Indians assimilated to white culture. Daniels emphasizes that "those people who are *generally* agreed to be mixed-bloods do not clearly form a distinct group in the sense that there are full-blood and white social groups.

'Mixed-blood' is a term used to describe all those who are somehow standing between the two major cultural traditions, *or* social systems, represented on the reservation" (Daniels 1970:212, italics in original). The Lakota word for mixedblood is *iyéska* 'interpreter'; indeed, such a definition is extremely precise insofar as the historical role of mixedbloods was to bridge conceptual gaps and interpret language and culture. However, recently the term *iyéska* has acquired negative connotations. Ernest Schusky notes that he has "heard fullbloods use the Lakota [term] for 'sons of interpreters' with all the venom that clearly makes it translate better as S.O.B." (Schusky 1986:65). I have heard non-Indians utter the term as a slur, to describe a person who has given up his birthright or is concerned with promoting his own self interests. In other situations, it is not negatively used and simply indicates a person who is of mixed heritage, but for the most part, when the term *iyéska* is used, it carries a political connotation – mixedblood with a kick. I have never heard mixedbloods refer to themselves by that appellation; they prefer the English terminology.

Historically, mixedbloods often were in a good position to hold federal jobs because "their legal identity as being an Indian brings them preferment in employment over Whites, while their superior 'knowhow' and knowledge of English brings them preferment over Full-bloods" (Wax et al. 1964:31). The federal government is the largest employer in the area, and this access to steady employment has provided economic advantages for mixedbloods, especially since the inception of federal affirmative action policies.[4]

One rural fullblood man, noting the ambivalence of mixedblood identity, stated: "Those mixed-bloods are funny people. When they're with whites they call themselves Indians and when they're with Indians they call themselves Whites" (quoted in Daniels 1970:213). An interview with a contemporary mixedblood bears out the fullblood's assessment of the essential quality of "otherness" that is the major characteristic of mixedblood identity in Bennett County. A tribal employee currently living on the border of Pine Ridge and Bennett County mused over his interactions in the "blue-eyed world," noting that in that particular social field he enjoys emphasizing his Indianness, while when in the company of fullbloods he enjoys playing up his whiteness. This mixedblood, who has a shock of silver hair and clear blue eyes, describes himself as a white man, an Indian, a cowboy, and a tribal bureaucrat. His internalization of certain aspects of all of the local social categories of identity was apparent as he effortlessly shifted personal pronouns depending upon the social context that he was addressing. When he discussed positive characteristics of Indian, mixedblood, or white categories, he used the personal pronoun "we" or "us"; conversely, when discussing social characteristics that he considered negative, he used "they" or "them."

Daniels noted that while fullbloods generally have rather negative opinions of mixedbloods in Bennett County, non-Indians tended to see them differently. In this view, they were

> better employees and often prove satisfactory as bus drivers and school cooks . . . desir[ing] the bare necessities of electricity and plumbing, and are likely to have food in the house . . . Mixedblood children do better in school because their parents, in a limited way, want them to make something of themselves. Mixed-blood politicians are smart enough to fool the full-bloods into electing them, but are basically corrupt and have no understanding of the higher purposes of public office. [Daniels 1970:208]

Again, by widening the focus, it is possible to view these surviving stereotypes as largely deriving from early federal policies. By entitling certain white men to the same property rights as Lakotas, the government created a niche for those who could better understand the meaning of federal policies and politics. At the same time, those white men often were able to garner support from their wives' families by using their positions as husbands in the women's network of relatives.

In contemporary Bennett County, mixedbloods are doing better than Daniels (1970) implied. Many people who identify themselves as mixedbloods have attended Indian boarding schools by parental choice, as opposed to by earlier forces of government-directed assimilation of fullbloods. In most cases, those schools are far superior to Bennett County schools, not because the county has poor teachers, but because it lacks resources to support the school district. Also, boarding schools offer students the opportunity to see other ways of living and exposure to a wealth of diversity not present in small towns (see Child 1998).

One highly educated local mixedblood man from a prominent Santee Sioux family told me that some students who attend boarding schools become concerned with adopting proper Christian behavior. When they return home, they hold non-Indians accountable for living up to the Christian model exemplified in their schooling, and consider it a point of honor, a moral victory, to be better educated and a better Christian than their non-Indian neighbors. Once aware of the dynamic, I could perceive a difference in some mixedbloods, particularly women who had attended St. Mary's Episcopal school in East River country. And yet, one such elderly mixedblood woman shared with me her regret that she had not learned the Lakota language, her mother's first language, because over the years she had become aware of what she had missed by not knowing it. As a child, she saw her fullblood mother lose her job as an elementary school teacher for using Lakota to explain a complex idea to one of her fullblood students. Life became hard for their family because of the loss of the mother's job. In some ways, mixedbloods see any choice to identify with the Indian side as losing ground.

I also found it interesting that some descendants of Santee Dakotas, an eastern Sioux group, who were contacted earlier by non-Indians than were the Oglalas, had opinions about their Oglala relatives. They considered themselves to be more "civilized" than the "wild Indians" in the west. This is an indication that years in non-Indian Christian schools had instilled in them a sense of social Darwinism that they, in turn, passed to their children. They perceived themselves to be a little farther along in terms of being civilized, and a little higher in the social hierarchy.

Whites

The most problematic social category in Bennett County is *wašícu* 'white person', especially when considered in its historical context. The first whites to enter the area were French traders, most of whom took Indian wives and were subsequently incorporated into Lakota society. Later, when the region was opened to settlement by non-Indian newcomers, ethnically and linguistically diverse groups flocked to South Dakota seeking the American dream of land ownership.[5] Due to the marginal value of the arid West River country, land was inexpensive to obtain (Nelson 1986).

One non-Indian oldtimer who has been married to his Lakota wife for over sixty years held her hand as he related their story to me. He is obviously a devoted husband, and I was touched to see the mutuality of their gestures and responses. He had been a poor boy living in Nebraska, the son of parents who had a small farm and a few head of cattle. He decided one day that he would work very hard to amass a small amount of money and then travel north into Bennett County, where, he had heard, Indian women had been allotted parcels of land. He knew that he loved the ranching and farming way of life and figured that if he could meet and fall in love with a woman who knew the land, he would be much better off than with a city girl. He found his future wife, a well-educated mixedblood Lakota woman, and they settled down to raise a family on her allotment. He was quick to say that life in South Dakota with his wife was a "step up" from the poverty that he had known as a boy, and that he felt blessed to have had the opportunity to spend sixty years with a woman who so graciously put up with him. He put a very tender human face on some of the "colonial processes of domination" that I had read about in graduate school texts. The couple's story reminded me that in Bennett County, as elsewhere, human beings are social actors and many of them make personal choices based on both pragmatic strategies and human emotions.

For the most part, though, in contemporary Bennett County, interaction between fullbloods and whites does not go much deeper than conducting business. There have been recent efforts on the part of some whites (especially ministers, law enforcement officials, and teachers) to encourage good old-fashioned neighborliness. One local non-Indian state's attorney who was married to a Lakota woman from the Rosebud Reservation related the story of a recent "friendship march" that was very well attended. The Oglala Sioux Tribal Council provided meat for a barbecue and the local whites provided covered dishes and salads. After the march, everyone gathered for dinner at a local park. The attorney observed with dismay that people were sitting in two groups – fullbloods and whites – with the mixedbloods going back and forth between them. This social event was an apt metaphor for relations among those three groups in Bennett County.

TWO WAYS OF KNOWING KIN

One major area of misunderstanding in Bennett County centers upon kin relations and responsibilities. Many non-Indians remark that Lakotas are undependable employees, often noting that they will take on a job only to leave after receiving their first paycheck. The most often cited "reason" for this repeats the stereotype that Indian people will work only long enough to buy liquor or a beat-up old car and then quit, often without giving notice. Braroe (1975) noted the same dynamic in his ethnography of the Short Grass community. While such stereotypical assessments add to the perception that Indian people, especially fullbloods, are lazy and unreliable, factors such as deaths in their communities, preparations for memorial giveaways, and frequent travels to powwows or to visit relatives living off the reservation must also be considered.

One fullblood Lakota graduate of Bennett County High School, who several years previously had earned scholarships to a state university to pursue studies in the health services, chose to postpone his last year of studies because of the death of his brother. While his brother had been sick for quite some time, death is always unexpected from a Lakota point of view, and he saw his family member role as primary. During that year, he helped prepare for the memorial feast and giveaway that is generally held a year after the death. His kinship-determined social roles of son, brother, and uncle took precedence over his role as scholar, and he never complained about having to postpone an important internship. Many non-Indian community members, as well as some mixedbloods, expressed concern that this fullblood youth with such great potential was reverting back to what they perceived to be a vicious cycle of dependency and undependability. They failed to perceive the active nature of Lakota kinship and the specific behavioral roles ascribed to kinship terminology (see discussion in DeMallie 1994). But a few who knew better expressed admiration for his commitment to family responsibility at the expense of his own career timetable. In the end, he completed his internship and returned to live in Bennett County while working for the Indian Health Service in a remote district of Pine Ridge.

A common theme for Lakota people, repeated almost as a mantra, is "It's hard to be Lakota." This is cited in reference to family commitments, investment of large sums of money and resources needed to fulfill family obligations, and the time expended in preparing for memorials and other ceremonies. Because of the inclusive kinship system that builds relationships between Lakotas based upon mutual obligation, funerals and memorials take up a large portion of their time. Especially in a small town, each funeral affects many people because the deceased often played many roles in community networks. People are more visible to their neighbors in rural areas than in large urban areas where, beyond immediate family and a few friends and coworkers, deaths can go unfelt. Each death is felt deeply in both the Lakota and non-Indian community because each death is understood as the passing of a unique human being rather than a faceless individual. What distinguishes Lakota and non-Indian funerals in this region is that the active participation of extended family members is more apparent and is only the beginning of long and expensive preparations for the memorial giveaway, usually held the following year. It is the function of the memorial to provide a social space and time in which the family is welcomed out of mourning and into renewed community life.

Relationship, both to kin and to land, was essential to Lakota people. In *Speaking of Indians,* Ella C. Deloria called Lakota kinship "a scheme of life that worked":

> I can safely say that the ultimate goal of Dakota life, stripped of accessories, was quite simple: One must obey kinship rules; one must be a good relative . . . In the last analysis every other consideration was secondary – property, personal ambition, glory, good times, life itself. Without that aim and the constant struggle to attain it, the people would no longer be Dakota in truth. They would no longer even be human. To be a good Dakota, then, was to keep the rules imposed by kinship for achieving civility, good manners, and a sense of responsibility toward every individual dealt with. [Deloria 1944:24]

Lakotas understood a genealogical connection between relatives, and "kinship being that important, blood connections were assiduously traced and remembered no matter how far back" (Deloria 1944:27). However, Lakotas did not limit classification of kin relations to blood relatives alone: "Sioux people speak of kinship in terms of attitudes and behavior, not genealogical connections" (DeMallie 1994:131). Deloria drew attention to the distinction made by ethnologists between the "social kinship system," which is based on the incorporation of friends, neighbors, and "acquaintances in white society" and the kinship system based on blood and marriage ties (1944:27). By noting the existence of such a distinction, Deloria identified a case in which ethnologists had made assumptions about another culture's categorizations based upon their own. Nonetheless, Deloria explained, for the Lakotas, the social kinship system was no less legitimate a form of kinship. As Demallie summarizes, "All kin relationships were 'real,' whether or not they were based on genealogy" (1994:131). He further points out that blood connection is never the exclusive defining criterion for kinship in Sioux culture and that Sioux people classify blood relatives with other relatives made throughout their lives.

George Sword, an Oglala who lived during the time of the Dawes Act, described a Lakota adoption ceremony called the *hųká*, which played a central role in the building and maintenance of kinship ties. According to Sword,

> The ceremony was performed to make the Indians akin to each other. It would make two Indians brothers. Or it would make them brother and sister. Or it would make them sisters. Or it would make them father and child. Or it would make them mother and child. When Indians became kin in this way, it was like kin by birth. When they were kin in this way they could not marry. [quoted in Walker 1980:198]

However, Sword noted that since reservation times, the ceremony was practiced much less frequently, having lost some of its importance because "the *Hunka* ceremony taught the *Hunka* [the beloved child, or adoptee] to be what the Indians thought was good. The Indians' way of being good is not the same as the white man's way. The white man's way of being good is now accepted by the Indians" (Walker 1980:200). While *hųká* ceremonies, perhaps due to their expense, are not held as often as during prereservation days, the notion of relatedness through adoption and the extension of kinship terms to others remains an important feature of social relatedness among Lakotas.

One *hųká* ceremony performed during a powwow in 1996 in Kyle, a village on Pine Ridge Indian Reservation, demonstrated that the tradition of honoring a beloved child and building kin relations with outsiders is ongoing. Honored on one boy's behalf were traditional elders and non-Indian teachers at the reservation school who had encouraged the boy to succeed despite his inclination to get into trouble. The family wished to honor those efforts and show their gratitude in a formal way. Traditional foods, such as several varieties of *wasná* 'pemmican', frybread, and *wóžapi* 'berry pudding', were offered to the crowd of onlookers seated under the dance arbor. Those being honored received Lakota star quilts, expensive Pendleton blankets, and footlockers in which to take them home. The crowd was then invited by category (veterans, "elderlies," children, and "everyone else") to come up and select a gift from the pile of quilt tops, dance shawls, pillows, rugs, household goods, towels, dishcloths, Tupperware, and toys arranged on a large blanket. People were not so much concerned with inspecting the gifts offered, or taking the most expensive one. What mattered was that something that was generously offered would be taken home. After choosing our gifts, we stood in line to shake the hands of those being honored, and the hand of the boy for whom the ceremony had been arranged. After everyone had taken a gift, the remaining gifts were distributed by family members, paying special attention to the elderly and the poor, until everything was gone. Those who came left with cans of coffee, styrofoam cups filled with *wasná,* piles of frybread to be put away in freezers for later, and arms full of household goods. Again, the important thing was that the family gave generously to others, building a good social relationship with everyone in the community who had gathered under the circular arbor to witness the event. It was expensive, to be sure, and the family was not wealthy. But to Lakotas, the investment of money and labor ensured something much more important than the expense itself. It ensured the continuation of community through generosity of both resources and spirit.

The kinship system remains the basis for Lakota social order. Historically and contemporarily, the most important Lakota social structures were *lakhóta* 'nation', *oyáte* 'tribe', *thiyóšpaye* 'band' or 'extended family', and *thiwáhe* 'family'. *Thiyóšpaye* literally means a group of lodges (or houses) and "symbolizes a number of relatives who live together as a stable group" (DeMallie 1978: 24–44). Kin networks made it possible for movement between bands, with the expectation that relatives would extend hospitality in socially prescribed ways. One's place in the nation was secure through the knowledge and proper execution of appropriate behaviors as expressed by kinship terminology. Kinship extended into the realm of the sacred as well, since "it had no prescribed boundaries; as a system of potentialities it structured and made sense of all human interactions and provided a comforting sense of orderliness to the universe" (DeMallie 1994:133).

In stark contrast to Lakota notions of an ever-expanding network of responsibilities and expectations stood the American concept of a tightly bounded nuclear family. The American kinship system works well only in particular types of societies and would be a hindrance in societies that privilege communalism rather than individualism. David Schneider, an anthropologist who studied the American kinship system as a symbolic and cultural system, has argued that "American kinship is an example of the kind of kinship system which is found in modern, western societies. This kind of system is particularly important not only because it is found in an important kind of society, but also because it is different from the kinds of kinship systems found anywhere else in the world" (1980:vii).

Even more pertinent to this study is Schneider's analysis of American kinship as a classificatory system sharply differentiated from other social institutions and relationships. By way of such compartmentalization, individuals are not of necessity required to act as kinsmen responsible for the maintenance of American society as a coherent whole. One may act – in fact, is expected to act – to better one's family's position in society, but without the responsibility of acting as if the entire fabric of modern life were part of the same interconnected relational network. For Lakotas, on the other hand, "there was no distinction between the kinship system and the social system" (DeMallie 1978:244).

The American kinship system recognizes relatives by blood and by marriage, as does that of the Lakotas; however, Schneider describes the former relationship as follows: "the blood relationship . . . is formulated in concrete, biogenetic terms. Conception follows a single act of sexual intercourse between a man, as genitor, and a woman as genetrix. At conception, one-half of the biogenetic substance of which the child is made is contributed by the genetrix, and one-half by the genitor" (1980:23). The product of such a union is an individual, one whose biogenetic substance is unique and completely one's own.

"Real," "blood," or "true" relationships, Schneider argues, can never be severed by law, although legal rights may be lost. While it is possible to have ex-wives or ex-husbands, it is not possible to have ex-children, ex-mothers, or ex-fathers. Parents may disown their children or put them up for adoption, and yet the adoptive parents, while carrying on loving, committed, and emotionally binding relationships with their children, might say that they are not the "real" parents (Schneider 1980:24). Hence, even within close and loving adoptive relationships, or in the case of legal dissolution of relationships between spouses or parents and their children, a distinction based on blood is apparent. Relatives by marriage, including spouses, are not related by blood; severe social sanctions are imposed on marriages or pregnancies deriving from relations between blood relatives. "By marriage" relatives result from the legal union (implying a sexual union) of two biogenetically unrelated individuals of different sexes.[6]

In the white American kinship system, an individual expresses even relationships with other family members in terms of distance. For example, one's sister is biogenetically closer than one's half-sister, who in turn is closer than one's step-sister; a first cousin is closer than a cousin who is "once removed," and a brother is closer than a brother-in-law. According to DeMallie, "the individu-alizing effects of white American nuclear family life were foreign to the Sioux concept of kinship" (1978:244). Lakotas understood kinship as an active, re-lational force. "They understand their own kinship system to be in striking contrast to the static nature of American kinship, an ascribed system of roles whose behavioral content tends always to be minimized" (DeMallie 1994:132). Relatives in Lakota society acted in prescribed ways as defined by their place in society. Lakota children could expect certain behaviors from their mother's brothers (referred to as *lekší* 'uncle') and her sisters (referred to as *iná* 'mother'), and from their father's sisters (*thųwí* 'aunt') and his brothers (*até* 'father'). Through respectful and deferential relationships with siblings and parents-in-law of the opposite sex and joking relationships with cross cousins and certain in-laws came the security of knowing one's place in a system. Negotiation of roles, duties, and responsibilities was not the norm in Lakota life. Rather than experiencing the social isolation of being an individual, Lakotas lived securely within a system with "demands and dictates for all phases of social life [that] were relentless and exact; but, on the other hand, . . . privileges and honorings and rewarding prestige [that] were not only tolerable but downright pleasant for all who conformed" (Deloria 1944:24). In prereservation days, those who did not conform would be forced out to fend for themselves alone on the plains. Those Lakotas were pitiful indeed in their social and physical isolation in the days before the federal agents brought "civilization" by way of social agencies that promoted an "individualism" that, more often than not, encouraged eco-nomic dependence on the federal government rather than the customary reli-ance on an enduring network of kin.

DeMallie notes that many contemporary Lakotas now do conceive of "blood" as the major factor of relatedness. He argues that "it is likely therefore that the conscious recognition of blood as a metaphor for kinship may reflect the influence of American culture and the innovation of a system of inheritance based on genealogy that was imposed by the Bureau of Indian Affairs and which has become an important focus of reservation life" (1994:133). Another Bureau of Indian Affairs innovation around the turn of the century was the standard-ization of surnames, which served to classify Indians in terms of the genealogi-cal model (DeMallie 1994:133). The standardization of "family names" enabled the United States government to trace Indian descent for legal inheritance of land, and it is precisely with this that the two imposed Euro-American con-cepts of biogenetic kinship and the exclusive ownership of private property converge.

Before moving to the next section, I must relate a conversation that I had with a man from Oglala at a diner in Kyle, a conversation that simply and convincingly illustrates how strange white notions of kinship seem to a middle-aged, college educated, fullblood Lakota man who is active and well respected in his community. We were discussing his plans for reviving Lakota as a first language in his community using the latest technology to record elderly people speaking the old Lakota language, to be broadcast on closed circuit community access television. I mentioned Hillary Clinton's 1996 book, *It Takes a Village*. I went on, for probably too long, about what a wonderful concept it is that children be considered society's children and that we all become involved in their upbringing and care. I asked the man, as only an anthropologist would, whether that would not be a great model for society. His response was long in coming as he considered his reply, apparently delving deep for words of wisdom. In typical Lakota fashion, he pondered, cupping his chin in his hand and, without so much as giving a hint of a smile, replied, "Well . . . *duh!*" His eyes sparkled and then became serious: "That's how we thought about things until they tried to make individuals of us."

TWO WAYS OF KNOWING LAND

The main differences between Lakotas and non-Indians in conceptualizing the significance of land were illustrated in Bad Wound's testimony during a meeting with government agents in 1883. He argued that "we [Lakotas] cannot even talk about [property] values, for we are ignorant of them, but we know the Great Father [President of the United States] always consults our best welfare and we trust in him" (Institute for the Development of Indian Law 1974:130). Lakotas valued land for providing the plants and animals upon which their survival depended. Land was not viewed as real estate to be bought or sold, but rather "represented existence, identity, and a place of belonging" (McDonnell 1991:1). Lakotas saw themselves as related to all of nature, as an integral part of the cosmos. The often-heard Lakota phrase *mithákuye oyás'į* is translated 'we are all related', or 'all my relations', and connotes kinship with all things, including land. One historian describes this simply, although somewhat stereotypically: "While the white man sought to dominate and change the natural setting, the Indian subordinated himself to it" (Debo 1986:3).

European attitudes toward land are based on philosophies of conquering and taming nature and, more specifically, in Lockean conceptions of land use and individual rights.[7] In *Of Civil Government,* John Locke posited that land could become one's own only through labor, and that it is labor that gives value to land:

> God gave the World to Men in Common: but since he gave it them for their benefit, and the greatest Conveniencies of Life they were capable to draw

from it, it cannot be supposed he meant it should always remain common and uncultivated. He gave it to the use of the Industrious and Rational, (and *Labour* was to be *his Title* to it;) not to the Fancy or Covetousness of the Quarrelsom and Contentious. [Laslett 1963:333]

Locke also provided justification for appropriating land occupied by indigenous groups and others who did not "use" it. Hall (1991:5) condenses this basic argument:

A person has a right to possess a given object [land included] if and only if (1) he labors for it or else inherits it or has it given him by someone who has labored for it, and (2) either (a) he uses it or (b) if he does not use it, his possession of it does not prevent anyone else who could and would use it from doing so. If either of these two conditions is not satisfied, then, although someone may possess a given object, he has no right to do so, and thus he does not own it. But if it is not his property, then, it must seem, others have no obligation to respect it as such and indeed have a right to take it from him and use it themselves or else give it to someone else who will.

Writing in seventeenth-century England, Locke acknowledged that Indians in the colonies used the land, but their labor was not understood as such by European standards, and so Europeans perceived a virgin land ready for the plow (McDonnell 1991:126; Cronon 1983; Smith 1978). But the plains, for the most part, were not suitable for cultivation, at least not before the introduction of modern irrigation systems. The arid West River country was best suited for hunting large grazing animals such as buffalo. Apparently missing the significance of hunting in the Lakota economy, one nineteenth-century South Dakota official reported that Indians were either traveling to the agency distribution centers to receive their annuities or else "in the hunt or chase, living the while in the open air, surrounded by a lot of mangy curs, a scrawny 'cayuse', and a number of dirty naked children" (Fite 1985:14–15). Lakotas were cast as part of a wilderness that needed to be tamed and cultivated by civilized Americans and European immigrants (see discussion in Cronon 1983). Despite that fact, settlers from the East and hopeful newly arrived European immigrants familiar with the prevailing wisdom that "rain follows the plow" came in droves to South Dakota.

As discussed in chapter 2, the Dawes Act came out of a philanthropic tradition and promised yet another "final solution" to the "Indian Problem" (see Hoxie 1984). The statement of the Commissioner of Immigration in the 1880s is an example of the thinking among many non-Indians of the day: "The history of the civilization of all the progressive races of the world, dates from the time of the establishment of individual homes by fixed and determined bounds, and the maintenance of those homes by the sweat of the brow. . . . No race or group of people could prosper under current Indian conditions" (quoted in Fite 1985:15).

Individually owned land was a foreign concept, with roots extending beyond the early colonial period. The imposition of the Dawes Act and the later Burke Act as instruments to allot Indian land in severalty, combined with blood quantum rationales intended to aid in determining the competency of Indians to retain their property or alienate it (explained later in this chapter), set the tone for the supposed rapid assimilation of Lakotas on Pine Ridge Reservation. The legislation was "the first comprehensive proposal to replace tribal consciousness with an understanding of the value of private property. The idea was not only to discourage native habits but to encourage Indians to accept the social and economic standards of white society" (McDonnell 1991:1).

Lakotas would have to deal with the realities of late nineteenth-century life, to learn to cultivate the earth that they called by the kinship term of *uci*, 'grandmother; mother's mother'. They would have to learn to think of their relationship to the land in terms of property ownership, lineal descent, and inheritance laws. All of this they would have to do immediately (even though Europeans had spent hundreds of years conceptualizing and internalizing this), as they learned to think of themselves in terms of "civilized," "uncivilized," "competent," and "incompetent."

In the late nineteenth century, groups of people came together in South Dakota, each with its own deeply held cultural understandings about kinship and land. Some came from a nomadic life on the plains, some came from the East, and many came as immigrants from almost as many different places as there were families. Federal land policy affected them all, but only one social (and legal) category of people – Indians – was expected to change at the most fundamental level, and to change immediately and without reservation or dissent.

BLOOD QUANTUM

The notion of Indian blood quantum, or degree of Indian blood, as an indicator of Indian identity has had a checkered career. The blood metaphor for identity has been both a blessing and a curse, depending on where – and how – it is invoked at certain times, by certain individuals or groups, and to what ends. It is a western concept that has come to define Indian identity, while at the same time perpetuating racial overtones and racial division. But now to deconstruct that concept might also mean to deconstruct the unique American Indian identity that has long been defined by – and based in – federal policies.

I do not intend to address that issue here. What I am interested in illustrating, rather, is how blood, land, and assessments of an individual's "competency" to own or alienate portions of land that were allotted through the Dawes Act became tied together, and how individuals were deemed to be competent to own or alienate their property on the basis of those factors.

Contemporary American Indian identity has been dually defined, from within the group and from outside the group, through the complex web of federal Indian legislation and case law. Felix Cohen addressed the problem of legally defining the term "Indian":

> If a person is three-fourths Caucasian and one-fourth Indian, it is absurd, from the ethnological standpoint, to assign him to the Indian race. Yet legally such a person may be an Indian. From the legal standpoint, then, the biological question of race is generally pertinent but not conclusive. Legal status depends not only upon biological, but also social factors, such as the relationship of the individual concerned to a white or Indian community . . . [many] social or political factors may affect the classification of an individual as an "Indian" or a "non-Indian" for legal purposes, or for certain legal purposes. [1971:2]

Cohen then offers a practical definition of "Indian" for legal purposes: an Indian "is a person meeting two qualifications: (a) that some of his ancestors lived in America before its discovery by the white race, and (b) that the individual is considered an 'Indian' by the community in which he lives" (1971:2). This broad definition was not the one held by Commissioner Cato Sells, who in 1917 made certain assumptions about mixedbloods.

Sells was a staunch conservationist and believed that Indian farming and grazing lands were pitifully underexploited. He believed that Indians should gain control of their land and the power to determine for themselves, individually, whether to manage their own resources or sell them to others who would. Such conservationist ethics derive from Lockean understandings of the utility of land and the presumption that the owner should use it productively. The government hoped to be out from under the trust agreement and to make their wards less dependent upon federal services.

The 1906 Burke Act was the instrument used in the declaration of competency of individual Indians and the issuance of fee simple patents (deeds). It was determined that competency, in legal terms simply the right to alienate property if one so desired, was to be decided on a case-by-case basis. A Competency Commission was established that would travel to various reservations and, with the help of the superintending agents, determine which Indians were ready to assume the rights and rigors of citizenship. In its haste, the commission certified as competent many Indians who were not yet fully cognizant of their land's monetary value. In some cases, Indians who did not desire to receive fee patents were forced to take them. Much Indian land was lost through fraud almost immediately (Prucha 1984:879–882; Clow 1981).

In a 1917 Declaration of Policy, with the full approval of Secretary of the Interior Franklin K. Lane, Sells set forth his plan for speeding up declarations of competency that would, he believed, hasten Indian assimilation into white society. He noted that:

> While ethnologically a preponderance of white blood has not heretofore been a criterion of competency, nor even now is it always a safe standard, it is almost an axiom that an Indian who has a larger proportion of white blood than Indian partakes more of the characteristics of the former than the later. In thought and action, so far as the business world is concerned, he approximates more closely to the white blood ancestry. [quoted in Prucha 1990:213]

Sells went on to enumerate six rules to be observed in carrying out his policy, the first of which is most cogent to this study because it set the norm for considering blood quantum as an indicator of readiness for certification of competency. He said: "To all able-bodied adult Indians of less than one-half Indian blood, there will be given as far as may be under the law full and complete control of their property . . . Indian students, when they are 21 years of age, or over, who complete the full course of instruction in the Government schools, receive diplomas and have demonstrated competency will be so declared" (quoted in Prucha 1990:214).

Sells believed that his policy would usher in a new era in Indian administration, and he was correct that it was far-reaching. He intended his declaration to mean that "the competent Indian will no longer be treated as half ward and half citizen. It means reduced appropriations by the Government and more self-respect and independence for the Indian. It means the ultimate absorption of the Indian race into the body politic of the Nation. It means, in short, the beginning of the end of the Indian problem" (Prucha 1990:214–15). But what if the Indian did not want to be patented? What if the Indian did not want to be assimilated? Was it in fact the end of the Indian problem – or was it just another problem for Indians, one that served to further divide them, fullblood from mixedblood?

The racial connotations involved in Sells's policy reflected the racial biases of his time. More importantly, according to Prucha, "blood quantum was taken as a norm (unless there were exceptional circumstances), and the 'white Indians' were turned loose" (1984:883).

Today the criteria for being considered Indian are based on blood quantum ratios originally intended as a means to break up Indian communities. One-quarter Lakota blood quantum enables county residents to vote and hold office on Pine Ridge Reservation and to receive free services provided to tribal members. In Bennett County, identity is the product of both ascribed status (especially membership in kin groups) and achieved status (particularly in land tenure). While mixedbloods play important roles in the history and politics of the county, as well as in tribal politics, they are viewed locally as marginal (Daniels 1970:213). Many fullbloods perceive them as "white Indians," sell-outs, and opportunistic traitors, while whites perceive them alternately as political and economic allies or "just Indians." However, mixedbloods are well positioned to make strategic decisions (such as whether or not to return their land to trust status) based on political, economic, or more personal factors.

Recently there has been a trend among mixedbloods to return deeded land to tribal trust status, thereby further shrinking an already strained tax base. Although boundaries and legal designations of real property have shifted over time, personal and group identities based on historical relations to land have not kept pace with these arbitrary legalities. Shifts in federal Indian law are viewed locally as capricious and reckless. They underlie deep feelings of distrust among Lakotas, who fear the eventual termination of their unique rights as a "domestic dependent nation." At the same time, non-Indian residents are concerned that their land might one day revert to tribal control. As chapter 4 will indicate, some of the more pertinent federal laws relating specifically to land in Bennett County reveal that there is good reason for such fears of betrayal and loss.

The narrative snapshots that follow will provide contemporary examples of the ways in which what we may call ambivalent identities are, although suppressed in everyday situations, strongly felt and defended in crisis situations. This is, again, a regional ethnography. View the following snapshots with an eye toward seeing how a region may be divided along enduring cultural, social, racial, and perceptual boundaries in times of crisis, but see also how the region may become unified in the face of interference by external social fields.

A CHANGE OF SEASON: RELATED SNAPSHOTS

This group of snapshots comes from a single roll of film spanning mid-December 1995 through spring 1996 and describes a turning point in my fieldwork. During the first six months of my stay, I had fallen quite unashamedly in love with the people of Bennett County and with the land that supported them. Many non-Indian people told me in quiet conversations that there was some racism here, but at the same time they wanted me to know that newspapers from the eastern part of the state and national newspapers had portrayed race relations in the county unfairly. Many fullbloods saw it differently. Over the years, extraordinary incidents in the Bennett County-Pine Ridge region had drawn significant and protracted national attention. Local people of all groups complained that reporters covering those incidents did not stay around long enough to get beneath the surface appearances of the community crises. I was told that it hurt the community deeply to be so publicly labeled as racist. While people agreed that there were some problems here, they felt that those outsiders came into town and blew things out of proportion. They wanted to be left alone to handle matters in their own way and to distance themselves from what most county residents viewed as intratribal troubles on Pine Ridge Reservation.

The takeover of Wounded Knee in 1973 by members of the American Indian Movement in response to then-alleged (yet undeniable) abuses by a corrupt tribal government headed by a mixedblood has been well documented elsewhere (e.g., Means and Wolf 1995; Lyman 1991; Abourezk 1989; Dewing 1985; Churchill and Vander Wall 1988). For the purposes of this study, it is sufficient to note that Bennett County was highlighted in the intratribal troubles because it served as a reluctant home base to certain FBI officers, AIM members, and media correspondents. Many residents – fullbloods, mixedbloods, and whites alike – related to me that they felt that they had been conceptually and unfairly linked to the strife simply because of their proximity to the reservation.

I did not witness overt racism in Bennett County during the first six months of my stay there. I did, however, notice that eyes were often averted or downcast as local Indian and white residents passed each other on the street, and that some storekeepers' eyes followed Indian people more intently as they shopped. But there could have been many reasons for that. To me, coming out of an urban context, the community appeared to be relatively well integrated despite its diversity, expressed in racial terms in everyday conversations. Only through experiencing this relatively peaceful region suddenly and violently divided did I finally begin to understand it. Unexpected events can change perceptions and clarify what often remains hidden in daily life.

Mid December, 1995

Ten days before the big day, preparations were well underway for Christmas. Main Street was decked out with colorful lights and decorations, and carols wafted out from the drugstore's loudspeaker system, cheering folks as they prepared for Christmas. The community, united by the spirit of good will, showed support for its children by turning out in force for school concerts and nativity tableaux in local churches. Proud parents and their neighbors took time out from shopping to enjoy the sounds of children from different grades in the ele-

14. Martin decked out for Christmas, 1995

mentary school singing Christmas songs in front of the drugstore on a cold but sunny day. Grown men wiped tears away before they could freeze on their faces and mothers beamed with pride for their children, and for their husbands who so willingly participated in their children's important moments.

From my point of view, everything seemed perfect, almost stereotypically so. The hometown feel of the place was palpable. Sugar, flour, chocolate chips, and nuts did not gather dust on the local grocers' shelves as women made good use of frigid days by keeping their ovens in constant use, making cookies, cakes, and candies for numerous upcoming church and community events. Women fashioned country crafts from bits of cloth and yarn while waiting for the yeast breads to rise and grandma's secret recipe "showoff" cakes to bake. These had to be perfect; people had come to expect familiar favorites to show up on the potluck tables at community suppers. This was not the time for innovation. This was the time for tradition, for fulfilling neighbors' expectations and knowing in advance what would be on your plate as you took your place at long folding tables covered with festive paper tablecloths. The holiday mood was seductive, infecting everyone with a sense of neighborly warmth that belied the frigid temperatures outside.

I accompanied a small group of carolers from a tightly knit community parish in Tuthill, an unincorporated town about seventeen miles east of Martin in Bennett County. The women had decorated buckets of cookies and fudge for the elderly residents who lived in their community and who were more isolated by distance or illness than others in the outlying countryside. We formed our cars into a disjointed snake that followed dirt and gravel roads, carefully negotiating our way around larger finger drifts that had thawed a bit during the day only to refreeze into a thick crust. Men, women, children carrying sleigh bells for accompaniment, and Alice the church dog tromped noisily through the snow to the doors of homes that were as well decorated as those in Martin. I was struck by the Christmas decorations that transformed country homes into colorful islands on the snowy plains and sensed that these lovingly arranged decorations represented real Christmas spirit for the residents, who were decorating for themselves rather than to compete with neighbors, as is often the case in larger cities. With a growing sense of excitement we traveled from home to home, singing songs that delighted us as well as the shut-ins whom they were intended to cheer. We were often invited in for cookies and a warm beverage and admired ornaments bedecking Christmas trees and creches. Tears escaped our eyes and I realized that the significant effort required in maintaining community was more often pleasure than drudgery.

After returning to the small church basement, we enjoyed cookies, pastries, fruit, hot coffee, and gossip. The Tuthill community was obviously a very close group that took care of one another, being bound by their relative isolation and several generations of family ties. Here, active neighboring was a part of life as necessary as breathing, and it was taken just about as seriously.

As the pastor and I were returning home to Martin, several police cars sped by, heading in the opposite direction, lights flashing. We laughed and commented that there was probably a pre-Christmas fight at one of the bars near the border between Rosebud Reservation and the eastern edge of Bennett County. Since the sale of alcohol on reservations is prohibited by federal law, a couple of small bars located just inside the Bennett County borders have become important watering holes for thirsty cowboys and Indians. There was some good-natured joking between us about a few of the more famous, and hilarious, bar fights we had heard about as we put the police cars out of our minds and turned our conversation to admiring the decorated homesteads on the outskirts of town. I remember being impressed by the sense of community in Martin and being moved by the real sense of Christmas, the first one that I had enjoyed in such a complete way in a very long time.

The next morning, one of the sociology professors with whom I worked at Oglala Lakota College dropped by my motel room to tell me that there had been a shooting in Martin the previous evening. She knew few details except that a local Lakota man had been shot and killed in the street by a non-Indian rancher from the Tuthill area in the early evening just outside the American Legion Memorial Auditorium, in full view of children who had been outside playing. She did not know whether or not the rancher had been arrested. We had just sung carols in his community, and I could not process the information right away. It was obvious that the police officers who had sped by us the night before, lights ablaze on their squad cars, had been heading to Tuthill to try to apprehend him.

The town was in a state of shock – it was so close to Christmas, and now ornaments and decorations seemed out of place. Faces reflected a community in distress, but that soon gave way to taking sides, making evident community fault lines not easily perceived by newcomers in the flow of everyday activity. Gossip spread quickly, and everyone tried to get the facts, but the facts differed with each telling of the story. The first impulse was to cast the shooting as a racial incident. Fears arose immediately because of vivid memories of the Wounded Knee incident in 1973 that turned neighbors against one another and transformed the town into an armed camp that housed both FBI and AIM supporters, many of whom carried rifles through the streets. That wound has not been healed. When I earlier had attempted to interview community members concerning that event, I realized that even twenty-two years later, it was still too soon to talk about it. Lakotas and non-Indians in Martin overwhelmingly agreed that this singularly painful event was extremely injurious to community relations. I heard the precisely worded response, "Wounded Knee II set back race relations fifty years in Martin," related from all segments of the community old enough to remember living through it.

The non-Indian rancher in this case was an alcoholic known to suffer from post-traumatic stress syndrome from his service in Vietnam. He also was known to have a bad temper, but no one in the community believed that he was capable of shooting a man to death. The victim was a Lakota man who worked at the local meat locker, was well thought of in the community, and was related to many local Lakotas. Apparently, the two had exchanged fighting words in the American Legion bar and the fight continued on the street after the bartender threw them both out instead of calling the police. The rancher fired ten shots, and the victim died while receiving treatment in the county hospital. It was a tragic irony that the attending physician was the rancher's brother, who was not immediately aware of his brother's role in the shooting, but who was understandably distraught when he found out.

Two days after the shooting, a candlelight vigil and prayer service were held at the spot where the shooting occurred. Almost a hundred people gathered, mostly Lakotas and a few non-Indians; the latter primarily younger children and clergy, to honor the victim of senseless alcohol-related violence. It was a frigid night with a bone-chilling wind and people were sharing mittens, scarves, and earmuffs as they huddled together waiting for the drum group from the reservation to arrive.

The people at the vigil were respectful and subdued. Mourners were given candles, white ribbons, and small ribbon bows in the black, yellow, red, and white Lakota colors that would be tied to the chain link fence across from the veterans' auditorium and stapled to the light pole under which the victim had lain. The Lone Man singers from the Porcupine district of Pine Ridge Reservation arrived with their drum and sang several Lakota songs; a little boy joined in, followed by several women who stood behind the drum and mournfully trilled in the women's traditional way of honoring. Someone lit a bundle of dried sage and a man said a prayer in Lakota. A non-Indian minister from a small local church also said a prayer. His performance was highly effective, much in the style of a shaky-voiced elderly Lakota orator when making himself pitiful before *Thųkášila*.

Everyone there felt a strong bond as they offered prayers and lit candles to place on the spot where the victim had fallen. No one was made to feel out of place. Those who had come were there to make a personal statement against senseless violence and the untimely death of a human being. Local and tribal police officers had quietly blocked off the street to allow the gathering to be uninterrupted by traffic and kept a respectful distance, hats off and hands clasped together in front of them, but still vigilant. After we had all stapled our bows to the light pole under which the victim had lain and tied our white ribbons to the fence, we quietly said our goodbyes and drifted home in small groups. Some remained for a while, weeping quietly as they held on to each other. One of my fullblood students who was related to the victim invited me to the wake the following night at the LaCreek district building located at the entrance of the Sunrise Lakota HUD housing cluster in Martin when she came by to drop off a pair of earmuffs that I had loaned to her daughter earlier. She also asked me to attend the second night wake that would be held in the Allen community, located near the northwestern border of Bennett County and Pine Ridge Reservation, some fifteen miles northwest of Martin.

The next morning, another of my Lakota students stopped by to ask me what I thought of the vigil and whether I knew what the colors of the ribbons meant. She said that some white people thought that they were AIM colors and were offended that they were stapled to the light pole in "their" town, but she wanted me to know that the practice was really a Lakota tradition that had been recently revived by AIM. She needed me to know that the vigil was not a political statement, but a ceremony intended to honor a human being who had died needlessly and violently as a result of alcohol abuse. But I did not need to be reminded; I had been at the vigil and knew this to be true.

Gossip was spreading like summer wildfire through the county. Some people in the Tuthill community were saying that the wake that was to be held at the LaCreek district office in Martin was, in reality, simply a cover for hundreds of Lakotas – whom some of the more vocal suspected were all AIM supporters under the skin anyway – to gather. Their theory was that the group would then head out to Tuthill to seek retribution on the non-Indians there. The minister and one male member of the congregation attempted to diffuse such fears, urging the congregation to view the act of alcohol-related violence as inexcusable under any circumstances. Still, for the most part, the community was firm in its unconditional and vocal support of their neighbor as they closed ranks in denial.

The First Night Wake

The Tuthill pastor and the elderly mixedblood woman whose mother had been fired for speaking Lakota to her Lakota students accompanied me to the wake. Our gifts of chocolate cake, dozens of cookies, and deviled eggs were graciously accepted by the victim's common-law widow and other relatives who were cooking huge pots of soup and making sandwiches to feed the guests. The widow wore a red sweatshirt and jeans and busied herself in the kitchen, graciously accepting the many gifts of food, and was well composed except when she would weep along with some of the mourners who came forward to embrace her.

The wake was held on the main floor of the LaCreek district building, and every available seat was filled, with people spilling over outside where they stood in small groups smoking cigarettes and making small talk. When we arrived, a Lakota Episcopal minister from the Allen community was beginning his prayers. He invited a well-known Lakota medicine man to offer Lakota prayers and to bless him with a careful smudging of sweetgrass. After smudging the coffin, tables of flowers, and himself, he set the braided sweetgrass into a Coke can that had been cut in half. His prayers were powerful both when spoken in Lakota and when translated into English. The message was that the community should put its anger away and should seek *Thųkášila's* pity, and be secure that there are laws – natural laws – and other remedies for this imbalance. He said to pray for justice, and things would work out for the best.

The district building is constructed in a circular shape reminiscent of the prereservation template for Lakota life. The coffin was placed in front of a curving wall that had been painted with a scene of two eagles on a blue sky background; in the clouds were suggestions of buffaloes and spirits. Along both ends of the coffin, extending the semicircle effect, were long folding tables. The table on the right held bouquets of flowers and anchored a silver balloon with bold red script that simply said "Goodbye!" Beyond the hallway entrance was another table of flowers. On the table on the left were woven baskets holding single cigarettes for the mourners to smoke, a guest register, and small bud vases with flowers, one containing a single perfect long-stemmed red rose. The elaborate spray of flowers on the open casket was interspersed with pictures of the victim's family and plastic figurines of an Indian warrior and his wife.

The non-Indian preacher who had prayed at the candlelight vigil rose to say a few words about the need to keep community anger under wraps by surrendering that anger to God. People listened to his Bible readings and the song that he sang. They were very respectful of him, seeming to appreciate his sincerity.

The mood was very unlike the non-Indian wakes that I had been accustomed to attending. Children were constantly in motion, running around and squirming. There was never a moment of complete silence, and people were free to move around and visit with family and friends while the service was going on. There was much coughing and sneezing, certainly a result of standing in the twelve-degree weather at the vigil the night before. One tiny Lakota child wearing jeans, a plaid Western-cut shirt with pearl snaps, and Nike shoes walked up to the coffin, went all the way up on his tiptoes, steadying himself by hanging onto it, and looked with awe at the body for the longest time. He seemed to be holding his breath, he was so still and thoughtful as he strained forward to see. Then, curiosity satisfied, he turned and smiled broadly as he found something intriguing in the pattern on the linoleum floor. That moment said so much: life and death were inextricably linked and naturally coexisting states there in the district building. Hope was alive in the children, who were not separated from death or from life, and who seemed not to perceive a real separation between the two states. They were allowed to be children – they were free to laugh, to play, and to touch.

The Arraignment

The next day, I left early for the arraignment so that I could pass by the place where the man had been shot. The hoarfrost was thick on the trees and the fence, where ribbons still hung across the street from the American Legion Memorial Auditorium, and the streets were utterly silent. Artifacts left from the vigil three days ago were apparently undisturbed, except for the multitude of candles that had been run over by traffic. I doubt that this was the result of an intentional act; life was simply moving on. It was a stark scene that frosty morning. I ran into a man at the nearby hardware store who knew the rancher well. I could see in his puffy eyes that he had been up all night as he shook his

15. American Legion Memorial Auditorium three days after the shooting

head slowly, deliberately, and said, "It's been a long week since Friday." It was only Monday. Friends of the victim's family were also showing signs of grief and disbelief as they selected housewares to bring to the second night wake.

Local lawyers, attorneys for the state, federal officers, and the county sheriff and deputies were already in the courthouse when I arrived. The sheriff and two obviously uncomfortable young state highway patrol officers inspected those who wished to observe the proceedings with a hand-held metal detector. Everyone caused that machine to beep. The Lakota director of one of the college centers was first in line and it kept beeping near his ankle. One of the state patrolmen said that he had heard that it might do that, but the officers checked anyway, to find nothing. I was next and was embarrassed because the metal ends of the ties on my coat and metal ornaments on my boots set off the detector. I asked the sheriff if I should take them off, but he said that it would not be necessary. I had a huge purse that the officers seemed too embarrassed to thoroughly search, and while my green woolen scarf was rolled up, covering the contents, it received only a cursory visual examination. The trooper on my right said, "Well, there's probably no big guns in it," and I said, "Never any guns." But he never actually checked to see.

The walls of the courtroom were of cinderblock; only the wall behind the judge's bench was paneled, and the ticking of the court clock was painfully

16. Candles and bows – reminders of a life lost

loud. I mused that the South Dakota flagpole was taller and had a bigger gold-tone spearhead on the end that looked better than the brass spearhead on the U.S. flagpole. Two deputies were positioned behind the judge; this had not been the custom in any other court hearings that I had attended. Many security measures were apparent, and the sheriff continually checked the doors on both sides of the judge's bench and at the entrance at the rear of the room, making sure that they were locked from the inside.

The widow entered the courtroom along with many relatives and family friends. There were in the end about seventy observers, including the wife of the defendant and their children. The state trooper guarding the rear entrance to the courtroom wore an uncomfortable looking bulletproof vest under his uniform. The attorney for the defense was very much the outsider, wearing a large gold nugget ring and watchband that were embarrassingly ostentatious for this county, and that caused the gallery to hypothesize about his fees. While the event itself was very out of character for the small town, all in attendance played the roles that were expected of them.

During the recess, those attending in support of the widow went outside to have a smoke and talk. When the proceedings resumed, the female deputy attorney general and the male Bennett County state's attorney stated that they would seek a premeditated first-degree murder conviction, which is a Class A felony carrying the possibility of death, or life imprisonment in the state penitentiary. After the female district court judge advised the defendant of his rights, a preliminary trial date was set for the day after Christmas. Since the date was relatively close, no bond was set, and the defendant was remanded into custody. The judge received and entered into the record a petition from the Oglala Sioux Tribe that the defendant not be granted bond at all. The defendant would not be home to enjoy Christmas dinner with his family. The judge officially adjourned the proceedings, and small groups of observers filed out.

The Second Night Wake

The round district building in Allen is similar in design to that in Martin, but instead of a painted mural behind the coffin, three Lakota star quilts were displayed. There were many more flower arrangements for the family, as well as plastic laundry baskets full of household goods for the family to distribute a year later at the memorial giveaway that would be held in honor of the deceased. At that time, the mourning family would formally be welcomed back into the social life of the Lakota community; until then it was time to grieve. The second night wake was held in Allen, where many of the deceased's relatives live. It is not uncommon for wakes to be held in different districts so that relatives from more remote areas can participate.

On this occasion, I was the only white person in attendance. I later learned that many non-Indians felt that it was not their place to intrude. Even those who knew and liked the victim believed that they would not be welcomed, "given the circumstances." They told me that even if they had received a personal invitation, they would still have been hesitant to attend, "circumstances being what they are." As a result, many Indians again felt marginalized and ignored by whites, even by those who had been friends and co-workers for years. Their grief, they feel, is invisible to non-Indians. Some non-Indian residents later asked me for details about the practices and symbolism involved in Indian wakes. I found it unusual that they had never been to a Lakota wake since they had lived in town all their lives and certainly must have known Lakotas who had died.

The fullblood Lakota pastor of the Episcopal church in Allen put out his cigarette and again rose to officiate this more elaborate wake. He was eloquent in his prayers and was himself quite moved as he offered communion. Again, there were babies' cries, talking, and much walking around during the service, but when the Porcupine Singers began their drumming, everyone hastened in from outside where they had been smoking and talking, from the kitchen, and even from the bathrooms. The singers began a series of three Lakota honor songs and were particularly good that night because, people told me, the lead singer was related to the deceased through marriage. People began to weep and wail out loud, but still in a somewhat subdued way, many men with their heads lowered onto their hands. The sense of community was overwhelming, and when the drummers had completed their honor songs, everyone immediately returned to taking care of the multitude of small tasks inevitable when over a hundred people had to be fed. Everyone knew exactly what to do because they had done it this way so many times before. Women began to dish up the hot soup, corn, meat, frybread, *wóžapi,* Jello, cake, Kool-Aid, and coffee for hungry people who filed by to pick up their unsteady paper plates and styrofoam cups.

My adoptive grandmother, younger sister, and I stayed late, but not all night as did many of the mourners. It was impossible for us to attend the burial the next morning because of the muddy gumbo roads that refused to allow my car to make it up the hill. We turned back to Martin and began halfhearted last-minute preparations for Christmas.

The local newspaper editor managed to offend just about everyone in town by referring to the sheriff's office as a bunch of "Gestapo" and "secret cops" for not immediately disclosing information about the shooting. Indians were offended because the articles implied that the victim had been to blame, alleging that he had started the bar fight and had gone outside of his own volition looking to finish it. None of the gossip that I had heard validated that supposition.

To be fair, the editor did gain some ground back by praising the candlelight ceremony as a powerful statement against violence on Martin's streets. On that, there was no disagreement.

Outsiders

Driving back from a post-Christmas holiday in Wyoming, I heard a report on the Pine Ridge radio station that AIM activist Russell Means planned to speak at the county courthouse steps at eight o'clock the next morning. Although he said that he had been invited by the victim's family, a person from the Porcupine district told me that a note hung in that district office said that the family had requested community support at the one o'clock court hearing.

In a radio interview that I heard on KILI as I sped back, Means stated unequivocally that Bennett County was land that was illegally occupied land by *wašícus* and that the non-Indian rancher had been charged only with manslaughter. In fact, he had been charged with five counts, ranging from manslaughter to premeditated murder in the first degree. Means stated that the man had been shot nine times; more precisely, there had been ten shots fired, with six actually hitting him.

In the interview, the mixedblood Lakota brought up the murder of Raymond Yellow Thunder in Gordon, Nebraska, which led to the 1973 takeover of Wounded Knee. The murder of Yellow Thunder by several non-Indians who received no jail time for the brutal beating that led to his death bore little relevance to the current situation. Still, Means promised "to be there, just like for the Yellow Thunder case in Gordon," and warned that he was "putting Martin on notice: when you kill another human being you pay – even though you're white." He said this as though he were invoking a curse. He also challenged the Oglala tribal government to back up its own people, then ended the interview with "I'm coming home," in a low and theatrical voice reminiscent of a professional wrestling "grudge match" advertisement.

The Preliminary Trial

I parked my car in a snowdrift across from the courthouse steps in front of the newspaper office about forty-five minutes before the trial that was to begin at one o'clock. A small group of Lakota teenagers wearing ubiquitous black and silver Oakland Raiders jackets threw snowballs at each other and kept looking to see who I was and why I was reading a newspaper while shivering in my car. They were on their school lunch break and had come, as had I, to see what was going on.

When I entered the courthouse lobby, there were already approximately forty five people waiting. A non-Indian reporter, the Pine Ridge bureau chief for the

Rapid City Journal, was asking the widow what she was feeling and whether she believed the shooting to be a reflection of racism in Martin. The widow did her best to avoid answering non-neutral questions, but the reporter persisted.

After a relatively uneventful court session, I was one of the last to exit the courtroom. The hallway was full to overflowing with people who had gathered around a man making a speech. For the most part, the impromptu speech had to do with his belief that there was little justice in Bennett County when it came to non-Indian offenders. His polemic was delivered in English to a primarily Lakota audience who were, for the most part, silently taking in his remarks. "I came here in '73 prepared to die, and I am here again prepared to die," he said, reaching for a response from community members, but most vocal support came from the younger kids, mostly from reservation districts outside of Bennett County, who were holding AIM placards reading, among other things, "Racism = genocide." By and large, the response was lukewarm; certainly there was no reaction to equal the speaker's vehemence. Some of the audience's faces did, however, seem to reveal a sense of pride in their silence.

Russell Means wore a crisply pressed yellow shirt, light blue denim jeans, a bolo tie, and a big black Stetson winter wool cowboy hat. He wore decorated rawhide hair ties in his long thin braids, many silver earrings, a massive turquoise and silver ring and belt buckle, an expensive silver watch, and zippered rubber boots covering his cowboy boots. His black satin baseball jacket had hot pink sleeves with his name stitched in shocking pink cursive script above his heart. The contrast between his appearance and that of the local rural community members was sharp. Most of the local Lakotas wore jeans, sweatshirts, and plain coats. Many wore tennis shoes instead of warm boots. People remarked that Means had taken time off from a promotional tour of his new book (Means and Wolf 1995), a lively autobiography and polemic on Indian-white relations, to come to Martin.[8] Means said that he had planned to return to the Porcupine district on Pine Ridge ever since William Janklow won the governor's position for the second time. He stated his intent to run eventually for a state office.

One local Lakota man wearing a khaki fatigue jacket and leaning on a wooden crutch stepped forward to call for an economic boycott of Martin by local Indian people. The activist immediately supported the suggestion, reminding the audience that he had "brought the Rapid City Chamber of Commerce to its knees when they forgot how important Indian dollars were to the local economy. They even apologized to the Lakota community over KILI in 1989." He said that neighboring communities would love to have Indian business and that Gordon, Nebraska would be happy to send buses to Martin to pick up people to bring them shopping there. I wondered why he would want to sup-

17. Russell Means at arraignment

port the Gordon economy, since not ten minutes before he had been reminding his audience of the racially motivated attack in Gordon that led to Raymond Yellow Thunder's death and the armed occupation of Wounded Knee.

A Lakota woman came to stand next to him and wept as she brought the real problem back into focus. Her son had been sentenced to life in prison for causing the death of a white man and was still in jail after 15 years. She expressed fears that there would be no equal justice in this case. Her humility and soft-voiced concerns were much more powerful than the activist's staged performance. He put his arm around her, pulling her close.

The victim's family began to weep quietly, the gathering broke up, and groups of people stood talking. I left for a cup of coffee at Geo's, near the courthouse, and found that many prominent members of the Martin business community were almost finished with their usual luncheon meeting. They were in conference in the small and relatively secluded area generally reserved for patrons to enjoy an alcoholic beverage or venture some pocket change playing the state video lottery machines. It was only about ten minutes after the call for a boycott had been issued and they had already received the news by word of mouth.

Conversations about the trial predominated in the main room as well. One group that included three non-Indians and a Lakota woman was seriously considering the situation. One non-Indian said, in a defeated tone, "Well, hell, I think he's guilty anyhow," and the others nodded in sad agreement. When the meeting in the back room ended, the commercial leaders filed out, dour-faced. They stopped at the table of four and said, "Means says this is going to be just like Rapid City, 1989" and "Russell says people should boycott us." The mood was one of measured alarm and something very much akin to sadness.

As I walked to my car I noticed that several of the stock boys who worked at a local grocery store across from the courthouse were busily shoveling snow, but mostly using the condition of the sidewalks as an excuse to observe the goings on. Noting that three of the four youths were fullbloods, I wondered how a hastily organized boycott would affect Indian people who owned or worked in local businesses. I wondered how it would affect the local non-Indian store owner's practice of extending credit to Lakota people who might find themselves down on their luck and between checks. Apparently other residents – Indian and non-Indian – wondered the same thing because the boycott never materialized. It occurred to me then that Russell Means had blown out of town on the same wind that brought him. Despite his promise to attend all of the court hearings, I never again saw him during my stay, including at the sentencing.

After several months, the trial, which wisely had been moved to a new venue to ameliorate tensions and to be secure of a jury beyond reproach (and free from possible repercussions), ended in a conviction. The rancher, who had been returned to jail in Martin to await the judge's decision, was finally sentenced to seventy-five years in prison. The verdict hung in the air over the stunned gallery, as everyone silently considered how long seventy-five years really is. The rancher would be eligible for parole in nine years. Both families sobbed and held their children close.

PARADOX: A REGION OF DIVERSE INSIDERS

This chapter has provided a discussion of historical, social, and cultural differences in the Bennett County region, highlighting in particular differences in worldview and perception that, by and large, coexist in a socially negotiated regional symbiosis. Yet at the same time, it has illustrated how local individuals are, from time to time, forced to give substance to an identity based primarily in historical understandings of who and what people are and how they believe that they are perceived by others in the community. In certain social crises, individuals must take a particular identity out of mothballs, put it on, see if it still fits, and try to stick with it as long as necessary. But what do these snapshots have to do with the ethnographic descriptions of fullblood, mixedblood, and white identites? And is there a theory that can stitch all of this together?

The answer is as ambiguous as the social relations here, and is dependent upon which social field one chooses to analyze. Do we want to zoom in for a close view of individual or group identities, or do we want to pan out to see the wider picture? In either case, some of the context is lost. To zoom in is to miss the larger social context. To view the larger picture is to lose sight of details that have strong historical, cultural, and social import. Static two-dimensional snapshots reveal actors assuming postures according to the particular context. Further confounding facile analyses of events such as those depicted in the snapshots is the realization that social fields interpenetrate at certain locations, at certain times, and under certain circumstances. And those fields are always historically and contemporarily fluid in terms of culture, and in flux in terms of social structure, since so much of the active personal, group, regional, national, and global uses of history are necessarily reinterpreted to address each new event.

Anthony F. C. Wallace and Raymond Fogelson (1965) find Native American identities to be based in blood and descent, land, and community (Wallace and Fogelson 1965; Fogelson 1998:44). Those factors are relevant to identity in all of the Bennett County groups, and in other places where Indian land and Indian ancestry have fuzzy borders. This analysis of the complications of Native American identity is helpful in understanding issues of identity in Bennett County.

According to Fogelson, he and Wallace recognized four separate identities that may be mobilized in certain social contexts, or as I have referred to them, social fields:

> An individual, and by extension, a group, may comprise an *ideal* identity, an image of itself that one wishes to realize; a *feared* identity, which one values negatively and wishes to avoid; a *"real"* identity, which an individual thinks closely approximates an accurate representation of the self; and a *claimed* identity that is presented to others for confirmation, challenge, or negotiation in an effort to move the *"real"* identity closer to the *ideal* and further from the *feared* identity. [Fogelson 1998:42, italics mine]

Here, Fogelson is speaking generally of identity, and it becomes clear that this may be viewed in individual psychological terms and also in terms of groups to which the individual feels connected. This analysis is especially useful in elucidating the problematic of being a mixedblood (or even, at times, fullblood) in the region, particularly in times of discord. Especially pertinent is the understanding that identities, when viewed synchronically in the narrative snapshots that we have been viewing from different perspectives, should be understood as extraordinary moments lifted from the flow of community events:

These identity components can be arranged in a lineal or ordinal fashion. Thus, in a particular situation a Native American's *ideal* identity might be that of full blood, a *feared* identity might be a Wannabee, a *"real"* identity is a person having three-eighth's blood quantum, and a *claimed* identity is a person with nine-sixteenths degree of Indian blood. However, identity components are rarely so ordinal and quantifiable. A group of protesting Native Americans might see their *ideal* identity as that of traditional warriors, have a *feared* identity as self-serving "radishes," a *"real"* identity as a disenfranchised minority fighting for their rights, and a *claimed* identity, claimed by black T-shirts with a distinctive logo, as active members of the American Indian Movement (AIM). The total image may be instantaneous, although micro-shifts in the relations and content of these identity components might occur in the process of interaction. Identity in this sense is primarily synchronic, concerning the here and now. [Fogelson 1998:42, italics mine]

With regard to Bennett County, Fogelson's observations are also appropriate for understanding non-Indians – ranchers, farmers, cowboys, educators, merchants, or the unemployed – whose families came from strong historical traditions of acquiring and then holding on to their land, status, and influence in county affairs. Their identities also shift since they have their own Western, frontier, and individualistic myths to live up to in their own eyes, and the eyes of others (see, for example, Butler 1994; Berkhofer 1978; Vine Deloria, Jr. 1970: 33–44; Philip Deloria 1998). Fullblood identity is also problematic, since it too is perceived by others to carry connotations that may be far from accurate, and are also situationally dependent. Identities are always products of history, situation, perceptions of outsiders and insiders, and, as this study emphasizes, depend upon the social fields operative in the analysis.

Regions have identities as well. In cases of outside interference from larger social fields, they also need to strike a balance to control outsiders' perceptions. After all, residents of Bennett County, for example, are not going anywhere; they will remain long after the FBI, AIM, Russell Means, and those who come to report on other people's woes have gone. The identity, for example, that served Russell Means so well in influencing Juniata College to adopt another team mascot did not fit the standards or the context of Bennett County. Here, county residents need to conduct business every day with one another – historical and social factors have made it so. They come together to fight wildfires because those fires threaten the local region on both human and economic levels. They also come together in the face of influential outsiders who only come to this place to pass judgment during its few extraordinary moments. While the county is marginalized, dare I say nearly invisible, in state politics and in allocation of resources, social dramas – the armed takeover of Wounded Knee on the neighboring Pine Ridge Reservation, a homecoming that no longer conforms to current national standards, a senseless shooting of a human being in a fit of alcohol-induced rage – bring outsiders into the region in droves. Those incidents are reported, and it is outsiders who have the power to set the regional identity in stone at the level of national awareness. Forever.

In a region where the closest Wal-Mart is over 120 miles away, people who love the land and the region and have chosen not to leave it will "lump it" (Greenhouse 1986). It's not pretty, but sometimes people just "settle." And that is how it is in West River South Dakota, whether or not it offends some outsiders' sensibilities. Conflict is a feature that must be endured, negotiated, and somehow dealt with, everywhere. This unique region is not unique in that regard. "Settling for" or "lumping it" need not imply that social change does not occur; cultures and societies are always changing, but perhaps more slowly in rural areas where human relations are intensely face-to-face. However, those changes must be relevant to social context, and must have meaning for local residents. Culture changes slowly, even if the idealized contemporary society reflected through images of "ourselves" in popular culture may appear to be moving at breakneck speed. Where humans live – emotionally, conceptually, spatially, and temporally – they bring understandings of who they want to be, who they "really" are, who they fear they might be, and why they claim to be who they are. Each identity carries meaning, the product of people's understandings of where they come from. Meanings are also products of the choices that people make in everyday life as well as in crisis situations, where it is easy to fall into culturally scripted roles.

FOUR

Legal Selves

Native American cultural constructions of space and place have rarely been accomplished in complete isolation, are subject to change, and can most fruitfully be discussed as products of interactions, competing views, negotiations, and struggles, current and past, not only within and between tribal bodies but also between native and non-native peoples. BLU 1996:198–99

Not all legal contests and contexts in Bennett County are as dramatic as those discussed in chapter 3, but even everyday concerns are underlaid by federal, state, county, and local policies.[1] While this chapter examines more ordinary daily events and attitudes, the convergence of multiple social fields is still apparent, especially in jurisdictional disputes that are both constructed and confounded by federal policies. Bennett County provides a typical example of the overlap of jurisdictional domains in a legal conceptual space called "Indian Country," defined in a 1948 Congressional act as:

> a) all land within the limits of any Indian reservation under the jurisdiction of the United States government, notwithstanding the issuance of any patent, and, including rights-of-way running through the reservation, b) all dependent Indian communities within the borders of the United States whether within the original or subsequently acquired territory thereof, and whether within or without the limits of a state, and c) all Indian allotments, the Indian title to which have not been extinguished, including the rights-of-way running through the same. [18 U.S.C.A. 1151]

Such ambiguous legal language not only generates confusion but can be redefined by courts with every new decision based on historical interpretations and reinterpretations.

Checkerboard jurisdiction (see map 2) leads to greater problems for Bennett County than the simple loss of tax revenues. Law enforcement officers arriving on a scene must decide which court will adjudicate a particular disturbance or determine civil responsibility for crimes and accidents. With several law enforcement agencies representing governmental entities that may not agree on the jurisdictional geography of Bennett County, conflicts, as well as opportunities for cooperation, naturally arise.

SCATTERED SNAPSHOTS ON THE THEME OF JURISDICTION
The following snapshots illustrate certain U.S. federal laws and historical events that contributed to complex and often overlapping jurisdictions in southwestern South Dakota. As important as these legal and historical facts have been, personal communication with various law enforcement officers, agents of the court, and private citizens has been instructive as well. Those interviews reveal fundamental differences of opinion regarding the proper authority of various law enforcement agencies and expose legal innovations and novel applications of law at the local level.

The problem of jurisdiction was clarified – and confounded – by one conversation with longtime residents. The following are excerpts from a taped interview with one married couple who were born and raised in Bennett County, and who previously had been publishers of the local newspaper for forty-four years. Their unique perspectives on this place piqued my interest in local jurisdictional disputes. Snowy winter days in South Dakota are especially good times for coffee and storytelling, so we spent a leisurely day getting to know one another in their cozy home. Our discussion was a lively one, the couple finishing each other's thoughts:

PW: What happens if someone dies right on the white line of Highway 18 where there is tribal trust land on one side and deeded land on the other?

MRS.: You are asking if they are just going to let him lay there?

PW: No, but I mean who is going to investigate? Which agency will take the case? It's so funny . . .

MR.: It isn't funny, it's horrible! Let me tell you a story from the early 1970s. Local officers called me one day and said there had been a brutally beaten body of an Indian man found not far off the highway in the field. I think it was about four miles west of town. The officers located the body on what they determined to be trust land, so I went out there and took the pictures . . .

MRS.: My husband used to take pictures for the police officers . . .

MR.: The local police assumed that the actual assault took place on the highway and naturally assumed that it was on deeded land where the state has jurisdiction. Well, then the state police investigated a little bit and also determined that the crime didn't really occur in the field. Initial findings seemed to indicate that the death had resulted from an altercation on the highway right-of-way, so the state had the responsibility to investigate. They investigated for four or five months or so and then they decided it was a federal case after all, so the state had to give up on it and give all their information to the FBI, or whatever – the Feds. Then the Feds investigated a little while and they decided that no, it didn't happen there, it happened on the highway since he'd actually died there, so the case came back to the state again. So then the state (and of course, this all involved a lot of time), so then the state investigated a little more and they decided that the state did not legally own the land on which the highway was built, they simply had secured an easement to build a highway over a piece of tribal trust land, so therefore it became a federal case. So [the state] handed it back to federal officials, and by that time two or three years had gone by.

By this time my head was reeling, but I did manage to grasp the logic underlying the final decision. The case had to be returned to federal authorities because the portion of the road where the incident occurred was not, in fact, deeded land and was not owned by the state. Such stories are not unusual in Indian Country. States with checkerboard and reservation lands are, for the most part, confronted daily with jurisdictional disputes among various law enforcement agencies – disputes that lead to costly duplication of investigative effort and delay in resolution.

Our conversation continued:

PW: That's why I don't know how anything here ever gets figured out . . .

MRS.: Well, and another situation that happens here all the time is that they'll be hunting for, say, some Indian person who's done something, either major or minor, and they'll go out to [Indian] housing and there's nothing they can do out there until they come out . . .

MR.: . . . no state authority. Here's another situation that most people don't stop to think about. The federal government handles what they call the "major crimes."[2] The tribe handles anything that isn't one of the major crimes. The state has no jurisdiction over either one of them. Well, the tribe has said "we don't want highway patrolmen on highways on reservations." But the U.S. Supreme Court has ruled that the tribe has no jurisdiction over non-Indians, so you've got no [state] patrolmen on reservations, you've got no one who has jurisdiction over whites traveling on the reservation except for Fall River County sheriffs and they are stationed about seventy miles from Pine Ridge.[3] So technically [non-Indians] can disobey any law and nobody's there who's got any jurisdiction over it. An Indian has the authority to make a citizen's arrest just like you and I do, but as far as any police officer extending any authority over non-Indians on trust land or within the confines of the reservation, it doesn't exist. Well, it's like I said before. The federal government has set up this situation – this no-win situation – and then washes its hands of it and says, "Now you people live with it."

His assessment of the situation is the widely accepted local interpretation of the federal government's intrusion into local and state interests, an interpretation with which local law enforcement officers overwhelmingly agree. Many state and county officers express concern, for example, that Indians who may be endangered or victimized on such highways by non-Indians do not receive the protection that they deserve.

The interview came to an end as the sun set, and the former publishers concluded:

MRS.: It's one government operating within another government, you know it will never work.

MR.: You can say what you want to, but it never will work. That is the same as taking a chunk of Mexico and setting it here in South Dakota. It just never will work. And there's nobody to blame but the federal government for having set up this situation up and saying, "You deal with it" and then they wash their hands of it. But this jurisdiction thing, it'll drive you up the wall.

MRS.: Well, and even if you wrote a lot about it, you know, if you write very much on it they'll say, "you don't know what you're talking about." That's what a law professor said when our son turned in his thesis about Bennett County. His professor said, "Well this can't be, this absolutely could not be."

I am not ashamed to admit that by the time we had concluded our conversation, I was more confused than ever. Nevertheless, over two and a half years of fieldwork had proven two things to me. First, despite the law professor's assessment, that *is* how things are with respect to jurisdiction in Bennett County. Secondly, theory and practice do not – and often cannot – dovetail neatly in everyday contexts. The glue that binds legal entities together here is a combination of local innovation and skill at creating a bricolage of disparate social and legal fields. The result might not be too pretty, but it functions well enough until it falls apart. When it does, law enforcement agencies just have to figure out a way to patch it up again.

Problematics of U.S. Federal Indian Law

The term "U.S. federal Indian law" is a misnomer and perhaps more logically might be referred to as "federal law about Indians" (Canby 1988:1). Very little in this complex body of statutory and case law has anything to do with the customary law that existed historically in the hundreds of separate tribal groups residing within the geographical confines of the United States. Vast cultural and social differences between tribes have been, for the most part, overlooked in an attempt to standardize statutory laws that still persist in treating "The Indian" incorrectly as a homogeneous category.[4] As a result, policies resulting from statutes and executive orders often are interpreted differently by the numerous federal agents serving the individual tribes. Those federal agents commonly find themselves implementing radical shifts of policy at the local level with every change of national administration. At the same time, representatives of contemporary Indian nations often argue that statutes and case law decisions applicable to other tribal entities must be re-tested in court reservation by reservation before being deemed relevant to their own concerns and treaty directives. One such concern might be whether federal allotment policies diminished the boundaries of a particular tribal reservation and whether settlement of areas opened to non-Indian settlers actually ensued.

The importance of situating each case in its specific historical circumstance cannot be overstated. The treaties that Indian nations negotiated with various European nations that came to claim their piece of the North American continent, and later with the United States and the Confederate States, were negotiated separately and form the basis (in western legal tradition) for tribal sovereignty. Such documents were signed by sovereign nations and enumerated agreements and mutual obligations between them. Since each treaty is distinct, it follows that each must be read as a cultural and historical text reflecting the particular time and place in which it was negotiated. It is necessary to pay close attention to the language and intent of signatories.[5]

Land Tenure in Bennett County

Bennett County may be described as the unintended historical product of a great experiment in social engineering. Thus far, perhaps due to the difficulty of documenting nomadic peoples who built no fixed structures and used materials that do not weather well, no archaeological evidence has been found indicating that any group of people occupied the area for any extended period of time before the reservation era, when the Oglala Lakotas were moved from Red Cloud Agency near Fort Robinson, Nebraska, to Pine Ridge Reservation in 1878.

To be sure, the Lakotas of Pine Ridge Reservation, out of which Bennett County was carved during the allotment era, were not of a single mind. For some Oglala Lakota political factions, reservations were protected places reserved for their exclusive use by the federal government, where they might live unmolested by European immigrants and Americans who were beginning to move into the area at an alarming rate, in violation of the Treaty of 1868. For other factions, the move to reservations signified a loss of independence and sovereignty, and the curtailment of an economy based on unfettered movement across the Great Plains in the pursuit of great herds of buffalo and other game animals that thrived there until they were hunted, for all practical purposes out of existence, to satisfy American and European market demands for their skins. This was not accidental; the U.S. government was aware that clearing the plains of buffalo that tempted Oglalas to stray from reserved lands would create a dependence upon federal rations. From the Indian perspective, those rations were at once a blessing and a curse. The same local federal agents who distributed rations and annuities "guaranteed" by treaties could just as well withhold them – or threaten to – as a way of ensuring tribal cooperation.[6]

As mentioned in chapter 3, the Dawes Act of 1887 was intended to solve two persistent problems: assimilating Indian peoples and opening Indian land holdings to settlement by non-Indians.[7] Under the Dawes Act, the government broke up communal land holdings, allotting parcels to individual Indians and holding the title in federal trust status for twenty-five years, or until an allottee could be deemed competent to manage his or her own financial affairs. After twenty-five years a patent would be issued, U.S. citizenship conferred, tribal affiliation severed, and the land would be subject to taxation. The patent holder then would be subject to state criminal jurisdiction. "Excess" or "surplus" lands were to be sold to settlers, often at extremely low prices and under generous credit plans – credit not extended to Indians who wanted to purchase some of the surplus land for themselves.[8]

In theory, Indians would be influenced positively by their new hardworking neighbors and, in short order, would gladly assimilate into American society. In the area of the reservation that became Bennett County, however, theory and practice once again failed to meet. Indians were told that once they were competent, or after twenty-five years, they would be given a fee patent on their land and could sell it if they so desired. They were not informed that some agents would defraud them through various methods, such as forcing fee patents on allottees by prematurely certifying their competency to fully understand land ownership and taxes, determining competency solely in terms of blood quantum, and issuing patents whether or not they were requested simply to clear title and be rid of the messy business.[9]

Hoping to increase the Great Plains non-Indian population, government agents, real estate speculators, and railroad owners enticed prospective European and American settlers and entrepreneurs, assuring them that Indians would soon become civilized, hardworking, taxpaying neighbors. Settlers were not told that the twenty-five year trust period could be extended and that, despite their hard work and investment, the reservation would not disappear. If early Bennett County settlers had known that their descendants would still live in a checkerboard county bounded by Pine Ridge Reservation on the west and north, Rosebud Reservation to the east, and Nebraska to the south (see map 2), would they have stayed? Could they have anticipated that approximately one-third of their county would remain nontaxable into the twenty-first century or that, come a change in political climate, the government might return their homesteads to descendants of Indian allottees? Many would have stayed, having already begun close bicultural relationships, but certainly not all would have remained. Others may not have chosen to come to this region in the first place.

The South Dakota Perspective

Lawrence Long, chief deputy to South Dakota's attorney general and descendant of one of the earliest settlers of Bennett County, is intimately acquainted with federal Indian policies and their effect on local residents. He shared his understanding of jurisdictional complications with me in an interview.[10] Since that interview illustrates the state perspective on the larger issue of the long-standing tension between proponents of states' rights versus federalism (the defining dispute in Indian issues since Chief Justice John Marshall's 1831 decision in *Cherokee Nation v Georgia*), I will include lengthy portions of it here:

MR. LONG: All the problems in Bennett County – in places like Bennett County[11] – are the fault of the inability of the federal government to maintain a consistent policy about American Indians. If you want to boil it down to one concept, the federal government has mangled the process from the beginning. When the United States was first formed, the U.S. Constitution had a provision that Congress basically has the exclusive power to deal with Indian tribes. That eliminated, for all practical purposes, the ability of states to affect Indian policy, at least directly. So the state of South Dakota, and states like South Dakota, I mean, any power that they had to affect Indian policy [was] abrogated when they adopted the Constitution and joined the Union. The federal government has had this responsibility for two hundred years, and for two hundred years they have been trying to unload it in one way or another.

The first way [the federal government] tried to unload it was to simply move the Indians west, [it] made treaties with [tribes] that essentially said, "If you leave civilization and just move out west, we'll make you some sort of a deal," see? That's why the Crow Creek tribe was trucked out here from Minnesota or Wisconsin or wherever they brought them in from. The policy was, "You go there," and the tradeoff was, "We will keep the white people out and we will protect you." Of course, to some extent they did that because there were old federal laws that said that white people can't go into Indian Country: you can't trade in there; you can't introduce liquor in there; and it was a federal felony to do any of that. "You [non-Indians] stay out of Indian Country, it's theirs, they can do with it as they like, ok?" Well, of course, pretty soon we ran out of places to keep Indians. The end result was that since the Midwest was the last area to get settled, the big reservations are right in the center of the nation. That was fine – well, I don't know that that's fine – but if they had kept their word about leaving this land for the exclusive use and possession of the tribes, at least you wouldn't have the situation that you have now.

His assessment of federal Indian law is accurate from the state's point of view, but the federal perspective differs significantly. The federal government perceives its trust responsibility toward Indians as protecting tribes from the many cases of intrusion and discriminatory actions on the part of individual states that historically have attempted to usurp tribal land holdings. The federal government's argument remains that Indian tribes and individuals must be protected in much the same way that states were protected from one another. The dispute continues. One may assess the federal government's actions as either outright colonial paternalism or as an honest effort to establish remedies for disputes that often occur between Indian nations and neighboring states.

Our conversation then shifted to a consideration of the Dawes Act of 1887:

MR. LONG: Of course, when they [the federal government] adopted the Dawes Act they flipped the [existing] policy on its head, you see, and they say to the Indians, "We're going to make homesteaders out of you." Ok, well, you can say what you like about that policy, but if they had followed [it] consistently to its logical conclusion you wouldn't have the problems you have now either. There wouldn't be any reservations because they would all disappear one quarter of a section at a time when the twenty-five year trust period ran out on all land. It would have all been allotted out and it would have run out on all lands and tribal government would have ceased to exist because they would have nothing to do. Because all the land would have basically been deeded, tribal culture probably would have survived in the same way as, you know – I assume like the Sons of Norway. It would have been a cultural-an ethnic group, but not survive as a governmental unit. I think federal policy was designed to eliminate tribes as governmental entities.

The allusion to the Sons of Norway suggests that here, at least, he was thinking about Indian tribes as cultural groups rather than as sovereign nations with a unique legal status. As is common elsewhere, individuals in Bennett County often do not distinguish between the very different concepts of culture, tribe, nation, and ethnicity.

MR. LONG continues: If they [the federal government] followed that policy [the Dawes Act] straight through you wouldn't have the situation you have now. This is the problem: they introduced non-Indians into Bennett County, and they tell those non-Indians – my grandmother, my grandfather – they say to those people, "This isn't reservation anymore. In twenty-five years all this is going to be gone," you see. *So they not only lied to Indians, they lied to non-Indians that they moved in there, too. They were every bit as duplicitous with non-Indians as they were with the tribes, and so they dumped them together into that area.* [italics mine]

Mr. Long identified a major issue in the county residents' resentment of the federal government. Many of the oldtimers believe that they were misled when the county was opened for settlement. It is interesting to note, however, that they recall the "old days" as the most peaceful in terms of relations between neighbors. Race was not a real issue then because in those days people needed to rely upon their neighbors for their very survival. Many oldtimers, Indian and non-Indian alike, related detailed and emotional stories of how they grew to love their neighbors through necessity. They perceived the major culprit in the breaking down of race relations to be the Indian Reorganization Act (see Biolsi 1992).

MR. LONG offered his opinion: Ok, well then in 1934, they adopted the IRA [Indian Reorganization Act] and, in my view, the IRA has been loudly touted for, and cited for, principles of Indian policy which aren't – I mean – which were not really, by close examination of the act, are not legitimate. One of the things that is loudly touted about the IRA is that this was some type of a reaffirmation of tribal sovereignty; in fact, you see, it was much less than that. If you do a detailed examination, what you find is that the Congress spent a considerable amount of time trying to figure out how they were going to balance the problems that a lot of congressmen saw were going to come.

For example, one of the things they absolutely knew was that to freeze the checkerboarding problem in time was going to create serious difficulty in the future. The Secretary of the Interior was given the power to reacquire land for landless Indians and put it into trust status to accomplish Indian land consolidation – was given that power to eliminate the problem of checkerboarding. He was supposed to – And there was a two million dollar annual appropriation attached to that bill that was supposed to be used to buy out the non-Indians and to move them out of the checkerboarded areas to create contiguous land masses for the tribes. It was an effort to go back to Plan A and to fulfill some of those promises that were made. [If] you had contiguous land areas, you wouldn't have any non-Indians living on Indian turf. Guess what happened? The Great Depression. [Congress] didn't appropriate the two million [dollars]; they never bought the land back; and they froze this situation in time, you see. I'm not going to attribute this quotation to myself, but he's absolutely right – "you couldn't by design figure out a way more likely to create racial tension than what the federal government did here. You couldn't figure out a way to do it and create more racial tension."[12] You know, it's bizarre. So the Feds didn't keep their promise the first time to the Indian; they didn't keep their promise the second time to either the Indians or the non-Indians. And when they actually did try to deal with it in 1934 . . . I'm convinced from reading those committee reports that they honestly tried to figure out how to reach some kind of a balance. And their solution was, very logically, "We've got to buy the land back. We've got to consolidate the Indian lands. We've got to make a contiguous land area for these people." Then they didn't have the economic responsibility to appropriate the money to make the Secretary of the Interior do it.

Now, you see what the federal government is up to is, and of course then they go into this termination business that they did in the [19]50s, PL 280 [Public Law 280] and the termination acts and all this other kind of nonsense. Which, if they followed that through, it would have basically got it back to, well, that was just another variation of assimilation policy.

In our interview, Mr. Long identified inconsistent federal policies and the lack of Congressional interest in allocating funds to low-priority obligations, such as treaty guarantees to Indian tribes. This condition has persisted throughout the history of relations between the U.S. federal government and Indian tribes. It was made clear in 1833 with Andrew Jackson's presidential reply to Chief Justice Marshall regarding the Cherokee cases: "John Marshall has made his decision, now let him enforce it." Since the same theme is woven through the perceptions of many law enforcement officers working in Bennett County, it appears that not much has been accomplished in the past 169 years with respect to Indian law despite all the radical changes in Indian policy.

Local Law Enforcement Officers' Assessments

It falls to Bennett County sheriffs, tribal police, state highway patrol officers, county and state prosecutors, and tribal and federal agents and judges to make sense of jurisdictional laws. Since this chapter deals with local understandings of jurisdiction, I do not include interviews with federal agents who are called into the area only to investigate federal crimes. Although they do work with local officers, federal agents are perceived as outsiders and are generally not privy to the problems, attitudes, and lifestyles of local residents. They certainly do not share (at least not officially) local perceptions of the problems created by federal policies. Still, for the most part, federal, state, and local law enforcement officers agreed that they worked well together and backed each other up when necessary. In this case, the operative social field is one of law enforcement: getting the "bad guys" off the street supercedes official jurisdictional positioning.

Life in Bennett County provides daily opportunities to observe jurisdictional contestations. Jurisdiction is often the subject of joking at local sandwich shops, not only among various law enforcement officers but also among Lakotas and their non-Indian neighbors. Joking about checkerboard jurisdiction is generally lighthearted, but it can take a more quarrelsome turn when actual events move neighborly conversations from a highly improbable joke to an incomprehensible reality. Although joking is common and an understandable stress reliever, no officer was willing to go on the record by telling any jokes to me in their entirety. Even when I explained the importance of joking for underscoring problem areas, several officers explained that some of their jokes were vulgar and that they would not like to share them with me or to see them in print.

I was concerned with learning what officers thought of their jobs and limitations, and what their priorities were. In interviews, they raised issues concerning available economic resources, interagency cooperation, persistent racism on the part of both Indians and non-Indians, and the interpretation and innovative application of law at the local level. One former sheriff[13] who grew up in the county and spent many years here as a deputy sheriff and state trooper threw his head back and laughed when he heard that I was interested in understanding how jurisdiction affects local people. To begin our interview, he related a favorite story from his time of service in Bennett County:

I was a state trooper at the time and joined county officers in pursuing an individual thought to be drunk because of his erratic driving at high speed. After a long chase, we caught up to him at the Indian housing development. When the suspect assumed he was on tribal land, he jumped out of the car and flashed me a universally known hand gesture – a "one-finger salute" – and laughed at us. Realizing that the front wheels of the suspect's car were on trust land but he was actually standing approximately six inches over the boundary on deeded land, I just walked over and handcuffed him. I remember that the guy just slowly shook his bowed head and said, "I think God hates me today." Later, my action was deemed appropriate when the boundary was confirmed.

After a good laugh, we moved into a discussion of law enforcement in Bennett County. The former sheriff noted that while there is a serious undercurrent of racism in the county, "the brotherhood of law enforcement officers is a bond that transcends race." He has attempted to recruit Indian individuals for whom he "would give his eyeteeth," but they could earn far better pay (twelve to fourteen dollars per hour at the time) and benefits as tribal police officers. He was "disgusted and ashamed by the pitiful wages of the county officers." When he was sheriff, deputies earned $6.50 per hour and were covered by an emergency hospitalization policy, but had no other health or retirement benefits. As he put it, "You walk out of this job with what you walked in with." Many of the dispatchers were Indian women who then were paid $4.50 per hour plus hospitalization costs in return for operating the radio and telephones, performing general office duties, handling complaints, doing laundry, keeping the jail clean, and bringing in meals for the prisoners. He observed that male officers are very protective of those female employees: "If you want to get the deputies mad, just give them girls some guff!"

Another result of insufficient funds is that the sheriff's department at that time had no four-wheel-drive vehicles, making it difficult for officers to navigate the many dirt roads in the county, especially when rain turns the dirt into a thick gumbo mud or winter winds blow fresh snow into large finger drifts that suddenly can block county roads for miles.

Straining this already meager budget is the requirement that structural changes be made to the county jail, which must often hold federal prisoners and thus must meet federal guidelines. According to my informant, "the state and feds set guidelines but provide no funds." Such federal and state regulations involve safety issues, open areas for exercise, lighting, plumbing, cell size, and the like, and many of the federal regulations are contrary to the logic of small towns. While a sheriff can request funds from the county to make necessary improvements, the money is often unavailable. According to the former sheriff, county commissioners working with an extremely limited budget do not realize that noncompliance could result in lawsuits with the potential for bankrupting the county. He noted that he understood their difficulty: "Well, I guess they [the county commission] could comply if they forgot about funding county road maintenance or any other city and county governmental needs. But if the county is in violation the judge could jump on them." He believes that a better use of limited county funds would be the construction of additional small cells, an impossibility given federal guidelines. When he was sheriff, a minimum of fifty cells was needed, and the cost per bed was $50,000. Costs have undoubtedly increased since then.

The former sheriff is concerned that at the societal level, things are far worse now than when he entered the force twenty-seven years previously. He noted a higher per capita crime rate in Bennett County than in Rapid City, the nearest large city, citing rises in alcohol-related offenses, drug abuse, robbery, child molestation, and sexual abuse rates.

The new county sheriff in office during my fieldwork noticed certain changes in his dealings with the public since he took office. When he was a deputy, he spent more time on patrol "keeping an eye on things." Now he occasionally covers for deputies who need time off, but, by and large, he finds himself desk-bound, dealing with paperwork, and much of his community work involves public relations. He is, however, actively involved in the D.A.R.E. program that educates youth on the dangers of drug and alcohol abuse. One of his main concerns is stemming the tide of "wannabe" gang members who, through popular movies, have learned the street attitudes of youths in New York and Chicago. Alcohol and drug use is a major problem, but even more common among teens (and more dangerous) is "huffing" glue, paint thinner, hair spray, and common household chemicals that are inexpensive and easily obtained.

When I asked how relations among various law enforcement agencies might be improved, he replied that cross-deputization would help. However, "the state doesn't want cross-jurisdiction because it's a mess. Tribal chiefs [the heads of the tribal police] have their own agenda, but we do work together pretty well for the most part." In fact, when Bennett County sheriffs and tribal police stop Indian persons suspected of committing minor crimes on the county road going to Allen, a primarily Indian town north of Martin, they allow them to choose whether they would like their case adjudicated in state or tribal court.

The Bennett County sheriff is quite concerned about how "the Feds" deal with stolen property claims on trust land. He feels that a skinny cow or a broken-down car may not mean much in terms of cash claims, but may be the single most valuable item owned by some Indians living on their allotments or in tribal housing. Theft of such property may mean utter devastation for Indian families that do not have telephones and need their automobiles – no matter how broken-down – to travel long distances to remote stores and health clinics.

The chief deputy of the state's attorney general further clarified the problem of federal jurisdiction over Indians:

It is the nature of federal Indian law that the major crimes, regardless of who commits them in Indian Country, are the responsibility of the federal government. The minor offenses committed by Indians against Indians are the responsibility of the tribal court. The "assimilated crimes," that is to say, minor crimes committed by white people against Indians in Indian Country is also the exclusive responsibility of the federal government. It is a federal felony to commit larceny – theft – on an Indian reservation; if you steal more than $100 – it is a federal felony. Among the people who live [in Indian Country], you see, what they have is of vital interest to them because they are so destitute. *But,* the federal government – the U.S. attorney general's office – has a policy stating that they will not prosecute a theft unless there's at least $1,000 involved. It eliminates their responsibility, you see.

One example of the seriousness of the situation is a case involving a non-Indian man who was living in a common law marriage with an Indian woman in Indian cluster housing (tribal trust land). He severely beat his common law wife, causing her great physical injury. Since the tribe could not prosecute him – federal case law indicates that tribes may not prosecute non-Indians – and the federal government declined to prosecute him, the State of South Dakota attempted to prosecute the offender. The non-Indian defendant's lawyer moved to dismiss the case, arguing that the U.S. attorney's office had exclusive jurisdiction to prosecute such cases. According to Mr. Long:

Our view had always been that we had concurrent jurisdiction – that either one of us could prosecute, and that had always been the U.S. Attorney office's view. But the South Dakota Supreme Court said, "No, that province is the exclusive province of the federal government." Do you think they are going to prosecute misdemeanors committed by white people? *No!* They will acknowledge that they have the responsibility, but whether or not they will actually do it, see, they just flat won't do it. It's just another component of the federal government's unwillingness to discharge its trust responsibility to the American Indian.

The tribal view of jurisdiction is somewhat different, but its perspective on community attitudes is not significantly different from that of other law enforcement agents. I asked a tribal policeman from the LaCreek district of the Pine Ridge office about checkerboard jurisdiction and interdepartmental cooperation. He replied that relations with county authorities "have been breaking down for about five years, since [the end of a former sheriff's tenure]. He was OK when he was a patrolman, but when he became sheriff, he stepped into that role and became a creep." He says that that tends to happen when deputies move into the sheriff's position. "I think it must be the role. I figure that there was a lot of community pressure on him. I bet if I ran for sheriff and got elected I'd probably be the same way." His opinion of the circuit judge is somewhat similar. He views her performance as consistent with respect to the race of the defendant, but he believes her to be far too lenient. When the judge first sat on the bench she was considered to be a "hanging judge," but now she has bent to town standards." He has a positive view of the state highway patrolman, who "stays out of county business pretty much."

In matters of jurisdiction, he goes by what he calls "the bible" – the Oglala Sioux Tribal Law and Order Code Book. This individual considers Bennett County to be undiminished reservation land since the tribe has not changed the language in the code furnished to tribal police. For that reason, he sees his responsibility as overseeing offenses committed by all members of the Oglala Sioux Tribe, and other Indians in Bennett County and on the rest of the reservation.

Tribal police respond to "everything that goes on here that relates to Indians," and this officer firmly believes that "all whites living on or leasing trust land should submit to tribal law," a viewpoint that follows if Bennett County is considered to be undiminished reservation land. He sees much of the problem of jurisdictional dispute here as rooted in the fear of county and state officials that the Bureau of Indian Affairs is taking over more and more of their jurisdiction. Ironically, and more correctly, another tribal judge told me that, in fact, the reservation had been legally deemed to be diminished.[14]

The tribal officer thinks that "there's some picking on Indians because eighty-five percent of the names in the court news are Indian." Subtracting names of tourists from the remainder leads him to believe that local non-Indian driving offenses are dismissed. He wonders about the true ratio of Indian to non-Indian offenders and suggested that proportionately more Indians might be taken into custody because they are more visible in town. In addition, while many reports of domestic abuse come from the Indian housing sections of the county, he suspected that there was probably a similar domestic abuse rate in non-Indian households but thinks that "whites might have more to lose by reporting them."

With respect to the issue of cross-deputization, the tribal officer commented, "it won't work because of hard feelings toward [South Dakota Governor] Janklow, but I would like to see it." Despite his belief that the tribe should have jurisdiction over whites in Bennett County, he notes that, for the most part, there are good relations among law enforcement agencies.

The lieutenant and three tribal officers in Bennett County get most of their calls from the small outlying communities of Tuthill, located east of Martin; Hisle, north of Martin on the Pine Ridge border; the Lessert community in the southwestern quarter of the county; the Blackpipe community to the northeast; and Indian HUD housing just east of Martin.

In the end, he sees the crucial problem as a lack of respect for tribal people on the part of the non-Indian community.

The non-Indian South Dakota state highway patrolman who spoke with me, while he established residence in Bennett County five years ago, did not really see things much differently from his perspective as outsider in many of the contestations. His role is to patrol Highway 18 between the Pine Ridge and Rosebud reservation borders and Highway 73 from the Nebraska border to Kadoka. He works alone in the county but can request back-up if necessary. While the state has jurisdiction on small county roads, those are not frequently patrolled because of lack of traffic and the need to patrol the long span of state highways. When this state patrolman is called upon to patrol county roads, he supports efforts of tribal and county police in difficult arrests or serious accidents. He also regularly volunteers on days off to work as an emergency medical technician for the county hospital.

The officer believes that his job training prepared him well. Following four months of training at the state patrol academy, he spent six months patrolling with experienced officers, enabling him to learn from professionals how to re-act in field situations. However, in these ten months, he received only one day of cultural sensitivity training, as did all officers. He noted that different regions of the state have different cultural dynamics that should have been addressed.

He believes that Bennett County is a good place to start out as a state high-way patrolman because different types of crime and traffic violations must be dealt with. One major concern mentioned is that tribal members need not ob-tain automobile insurance or a driver's license to drive on the reservation, but must have both if entering state land. Many people are afraid to leave the reser-vation for fear that they will be picked up for state traffic offenses and heavily fined for not being licensed or insured; this officer believes that the Oglala Sioux Tribal Council contributes to the problem by not requiring what the state requires.[15]

The highway patrolman is often invited by the tribe to lecture on auto and bicycle safety and is usually well received on the reservation. Regarding those who do not welcome him, he noted that "any animosity is usually politically motivated. I consider it *pro forma* and not personal at all." He added:

Some folks would like to see the HP [state highway patrol] on reservation because there is a kinship-based overturn in government. The new faction generally releases unrelated officers from the tribal police force, resulting in a perpetually new and inexperienced force that does not deal well with arresting their own family members. Some tribal police have criminal records varying from misdemeanors to felonies and have warrants for their arrest if they cross the reservation borders.

He pointed out the fact that tribal administration is elected every two years and that they barely get a feel for the job before they are replaced. Only once has a person held the office for two consecutive terms, and that was Dick Wilson, who was reelected after his controversial tenure during the events at Wounded Knee in 1973.

When asked how tribal officers compare to other jurisdictional entities, he responded that, due to constant turnover of personnel, they are basically an inexperienced force. "But they have really excellent equipment and excellent training. They go to Arizona to train at the BIA officer training facility, but must sometimes wait up to six months to get into it. Meanwhile, they are working on the reservation. Untrained officers are given a gun and told to go on patrol, often with no partner. That allows them to internalize bad habits before they are properly trained."

He noted that Bennett County officers receive far less training than highway patrol officers and operate under extremely restrictive budgets. "Six or seven dollars an hour cannot keep them. The Highway Patrol starts at ten dollars per hour and ten dollars per diem. We have medical, dental, and retirement plans. Bennett County voters turned down state insurance for law enforcement because of an already steep tax rate. This area has the third highest per capita crime in the state." The county thus depends upon only one state highway patrol officer, who works only five days a week, one sheriff and five deputies, and a few tribal police officers.

His assessment of the situation is that state highway patrol officers receive better training, higher pay, and better benefits than the county sheriffs and deputies, and that conditions have been getting worse for county law enforcement. At the same time, he feels that it is safe to walk around town at night since there are very few violent crimes against people in the streets. He sees burglary, robbery, and domestic rape as the prevalent local crimes.

In the court section of the local newspaper, one finds an apparently unbalanced crime rate with respect to race – many more fullblood names appear in the column as accused perpetrators of crime. The highway patrol officer emphasized that "ninety percent of *reported* crime was Indian." He believes that many non-Indians simply do not report crimes in the white community. "Non-Indians have more to lose by reporting; there is some evidence that victims of domestic abuse, for example, will seek medical attention in Rapid City or Valentine, Nebraska, because of how gossip gets out. Reputation is very important." He said it interested him that he gets less "flack" from Indians than from non-Indians. "When I pull some non-Indian over, I am often asked, 'Why aren't you out busting Indians?' " He has seen some decline in such prejudicial attitudes, but believes that to eradicate them completely, there must be a better balance in property ownership, and that more Indians must involve themselves in city and county politics.

This officer recently left Bennett County because he was "burned out on jurisdictional problems" and "tired of being accused of being a racist by Indians and non-Indians alike." While he enjoys his new position, he misses the diversity of Bennett County, his friends there, and his volunteer work as an emergency medical technician. He also noted that since his departure, there has been no state highway patrol coverage in this area.

To complement information provided by local law enforcement officers, I solicited the opinion of one of the local magistrates, whose function it is to preside over the initial appearance of any suspected criminal and judge Class II misdemeanors and petty offenses. Their duties include officially charging suspects, informing them of their rights, "getting a case started through court process," and setting bail according to circuit court guidelines. No formal legal training is required to perform the duties of magistrate or court clerk in Bennett County.

Since magistrate court is not a court of record, "it runs like a night court." It is possible to "informally suggest that the defendant pay [a traffic fine]; [we] couldn't do that if it were a court of record." Court is held twice daily, in the early morning and late afternoon, with an additional session on Thursday evening. There are usually many more cases on Saturday and Sunday mornings because of weekend drinking. According to the magistrate, offenders are predominantly Indian people because, he believes, there is more alcohol abuse among that segment of the population. Other than traffic violations, alcohol abuse and indigence are the predominant offenses. He estimated that "ninety-five percent of the cases [that come before him] are alcohol-related. They're either drunk or trying to get money to get drunk." The magistrate did not mention the fact that Indian people who drink are often far more visible than non-Indians in the same condition. Much of this can be attributed to the fact that Indians must first travel off the reservation to buy alcohol, and then consume that alcohol before returning to the reservation or HUD housing in Bennett County because it is illegal to sell or consume alcohol on Indian land. People residing on Indian land cannot legally enjoy a couple of beers while watching a game on TV in the privacy of their own homes. Public consumption of alcoholic beverages, and the related traffic offenses and accidents, finally renders visible in a negative way those who are often invisible in Bennett County, while the federal law that caused such a condition in the first place is forgotten.

The magistrate related that the lack of cross-deputization is a shortcoming because the state and tribe disagree on jurisdictional boundaries. Most of the local tribal police were born and raised in this community, and he has noticed that tribal police and county officers tend to "play out their perceived roles" with one another. Despite that fact, the officers have developed an "off the record relationship between jurisdictions. There's a different set of rules in Bennett County; we have to work with them." He then related a case in which a "deceased person was laying on a gravel road and was dragged over the road's [imaginary] center line." Because of a minor shift in the position of the body, the case "wound up in federal court instead of tribal." It should be mentioned that this was not the same case that the former newspaper publishers related to me.

There is room for the exercise of discretion on the part of both tribal and county law enforcement officers. As the magistrate noted, "everyone answers calls about [a certain local Lakota family] because they all want to fry that family. They will pick the agency that refers the case to the harshest court for them [because they are known drug dealers and a nuisance to the community at large]."

Jurisdiction: Between a Rock and a Hard Place

This snapshot from Bennett County illustrates the dynamics of overlapping jurisdictional domains and the problem of contested jurisdictional boundaries in Indian Country, carrying potentially serious implications for Indians and non-Indians alike. One evening, tribal police from LaCreek, the district of Pine Ridge that lies within Bennett County, responded to a report of several youths driving drunk and speeding along a gravel road that heads north out of town toward an Indian community. The county sheriff also answered the call. The youths, Oglala Lakotas, had been apprehended on the gravel road at a place with deeded land on one side and trust land on the other. The tribal officers believed that they had jurisdiction and, over the county sheriff's vigorous objections, the youths were taken into custody by tribal police and placed in jail on Pine Ridge Reservation. The juvenile offenders' parents turned to county law enforcement officers for advice about how to proceed with a civil suit against the tribal officers for false arrest, kidnapping, and false imprisonment.

Jurisdictional matters are always complicated when taxable and nontaxable land lie across a road from one another. Since land status extends to the center line of the road, the direction in which an offender is traveling must be considered. It is not uncommon for jurisdictional calls to come down literally to inches; independent surveyors must be called in for those occasions. Such scenarios happen more frequently than one might expect.

For tribal police, the jurisdictional issue was far from clear. In fact, the Oglala Sioux Tribal Law and Code Book requires tribal police to deal with all Indians and non-Indians involved in criminal acts on Bennett County land, since the code refers to Bennett County as undiminished reservation land. Exceptions to the rule are offenses enumerated in the Major Crimes Act (18 U.S.C. 1153).[16] For such offenses, the tribe retains concurrent jurisdiction with federal courts. The following language appears in the Oglala Sioux Tribal Law and Code Book:

> Pursuant to Article I of the Constitution and By-Laws of the Oglala Sioux Tribe, the Tribe retains jurisdiction of the territory within the exterior boundaries of the Pine Ridge Indian Reservation as defined by Congress on March 2, 1889. . . . As an entity of the Oglala Sioux Tribe, the Public Safety Department and its officers are under *obligation to comply* with the Oglala Sioux Tribe's Constitution, OST Code and Procedures governing the protection of the boundaries of the Pine Ridge Indian Reservation and

the protection of the rights of the residents within these exterior boundaries as well. [italics mine]

The following two paragraphs note the requirement that tribal officers document all actions made by South Dakota and county authorities. In addition, they are to inform state and county law enforcement personnel that "absent authority from Congress to patrol [the reservation], their [Bennett County] jurisdiction is limited":

. . . The Oglala Sioux Tribal Court takes the position that once Congress has established an Indian Reservation, all land within the boundaries remain a part of the Reservation including those portions of Jackson [Washabaugh] and Bennett Counties which are within the Reservation boundaries.

Until Congress has separated these counties from the Pine Ridge Indian Reservation, the Public Safety Department shall continue to assert Tribal jurisdiction. [Preamble to an Oglala Sioux Tribal Court Standing Order (February 14, 1986) included in the OST Tribal Code and Procedures]

In other words, while the Oglala Sioux Tribe generally concedes that the county was opened for settlement and organized as a county independent of Pine Ridge, it considers its reservation boundaries still intact, with all of Bennett County seen as reservation land in terms of jurisdiction over Indians.

In 1975, two pertinent cases were decided in the U.S. Eighth Circuit Court of Appeals that addressed the question of diminishment of Pine Ridge and Rosebud reservations.[17] The circuit court found that both had been diminished, but only the Rosebud case was selected to be heard by the U.S. Supreme Court, which upheld the lower court's decision. Pine Ridge tribal officials argued that although they were not parties to the Rosebud case, the Supreme Court decision spoke only obliquely to Pine Ridge circumstances. Based on that reasoning, the Oglala Sioux Tribe left its tribal code unchanged, claiming criminal jurisdiction over Indians in Bennett County. However, I was told by one tribal judge that, in his opinion, the two 1975 cases *have* been decided and that Pine Ridge Reservation *has,* in fact, been diminished.

Should the Pine Ridge case concerning the juveniles ever reach the U.S. Supreme Court, the court could determine once and for all whether the reservation has been diminished. While the outcome of such a suit might satisfy some immediate monetary concerns for their families, a decision in the courts could have far-reaching implications for all of Indian Country; it could allow the United States to hold tribal officials responsible for cash settlements of civil rights abuses of individual tribal members. Such a decision would essentially reverse the 1978 decision in *Santa Clara Pueblo v Martinez* (Prucha 1990:287–88)[18] and result in a diminishment of tribal sovereignty on a national level. In essence, Indians who believe that their civil rights have been violated by the tribe are currently in the unenviable position of deciding whether it is worth seeking personal remuneration at the expense of being an agent in the diminishment of sovereignty of all tribes.

Several common themes emerged from interviews with various law enforcement officers, displaying a fairly consistent understanding of interagency jurisdictional disputes and community attitudes. Some of those themes were: (1) the fact of racism in Bennett County; (2) the fairly good working relationship among local law enforcement officers; (3) the relative visibility and invisibility of Indian and non-Indian crime; (4) the discrepancies in economic and educational resources of law enforcement agencies; and (5) the broad flexibility in the application of law at the local level.

With respect to the theme of racism, it is necessary to move beyond facile catchall terminology in order to examine why community contests were couched in racial terms in the first place. Several questions emerge: What internalized boundaries affect personal and group identity in Bennett County? Are the problems that exist here really caused by race, or do they derive from a rural poverty subjected to constantly worsening economic pressures?

It is necessary to pause here and consider that funds promised by the federal government for expenses such as county jail improvements or the operation of the Bureau of Indian Affairs (which includes tribal police) cannot be counted on. They are included in the annual federal budget and funded (or only partially funded, or left unfunded) by Congressional appropriations. The federal fiscal emergency that closed all "non-essential" governmental agencies in 1995 had an immediate and frightening effect on Bennett County. Many Indians and non-Indians in this county – one of the poorest in the state – depend upon federal funds provided through child welfare entitlements, social security programs, numerous agricultural programs and farm subsidies, and Indian programs. During the 1995 crisis, nearly all federal offices in the county were deemed to be "non-essential," and Indians fared the worst since the federal government acts as a trustee for their estate – the "non-essential" Bureau of Indian Affairs clerks who process checks had been furloughed, causing an extreme fiscal emergency on the reservation, and in Bennett County. This is another example of how decisions made in national spheres affect internal relations within local social fields.

It is common knowledge that economic crises compromise race relations when groups are forced to compete for diminishing resources. During my stay in Bennett County, severe cuts in federal programs were the most frequent topic of conversation in local diners. At the same time, Governor Janklow instituted a twenty percent property tax cut, and there is currently no state income tax. To compensate for the resulting loss of state revenue, he made deep cuts in state government expenditures by reducing government jobs and discontinuing services; many local people suffered as a result. Anger festers as local economic stress causes people to fight among themselves for resources that are becoming even more limited.

It is almost impossible for county residents to separate the two distinct but related legal concepts represented by the differently shaded areas on map 2. Land tenure and jurisdiction are often jumbled together in the perceptions of local residents, but each carries its own specific meaning. Owning taxable land indicates that a person is responsible, hardworking, and pays his own share of county services. On the other hand, owning nontaxable land signifies incompetence, laziness, or if that land is held in tribal trust, "getting a free ride at the taxpayers' expense." The creation of a national wildlife conservation area, which removed some of the most productive land in the county from the tax base, did not help the perception of a one-sided intrusion by the federal government into county affairs. Those perceptions are mobilized during times of dispute, often bringing a moral tone to legal contests.

The jurisdictional arrangement again splits the county into familiar factions, still expressed in terms of race and competency. In addition, law enforcement is complicated by very different understandings of jurisdictional obligations on the part of county sheriffs, state patrolmen, Bureau of Indian Affairs officers, and occasionally, the FBI. As Lawrence Long said, relating anthropologist Thomas Biolsi's position, "you couldn't by design figure out a way more likely to create racial tension than what the federal government did [in Bennett County]."[19]

There are extremely high stakes in Bennett County – stakes that until 1987 included a potential uprooting of certain long-established non-Indian taxpayers (see LaFave 1984). For the first time, non-Indians, like Indians so many years ago, were faced with the potential of forced relocation. More importantly, and despite the 1987 decision of the Eighth U.S. Circuit Court of Appeals concerning what came to be known as "2415 cases,"[20] many non-Indian ranchers and farmers *continue* to fear that the very real possibility of eventual relocation exists. They, too, have become used to major shifts in federal policy that come like clockwork every twenty or thirty years, following alternating conservative and liberal ideological shifts in the national social field. However, in the area of Indian affairs, recovery from conservative swings is always slower.

The question of the legal status of Bennett County land has left a legacy of doubt and fear that is always just below the surface when neighbors interact on Main Street. A status quo of ambivalence and ambiguity in jurisdictional matters causes tension between community members in times of change or crisis, preventing them from seeing each other in terms other than racial. Any jurisdictional dispute tends to polarize citizens in Bennett County since, by its very nature, it highlights differences in race, social class, and perceived competency. Finally, "legitimate" taxpayers, many of whom fear that their land may eventually revert to reservation jurisdiction by one shift of federal policy or another, can only hold their breath, cross their fingers, and wait.

FIVE

Bennett County as Community

The banalities and distractions of the way we live now lead us, often enough, to lose sight of how much it matters just where we are and what it is like to be there. The ethnography of place is, if anything, more critical for those who, listening to forests or experiencing stones, know better. GEERTZ 1996:262

THE WILD HORSE BUTTE POWWOW

The dance arbor had been prepared. Fresh pine branches had been cut and laid over a white wooden frame to provide welcome shade from the August sun. Men were busy with last-minute problems involving the complicated system of speakers attached to the arbor. There was little conversation among them – they knew exactly what their jobs entailed. Younger men and boys watched and learned so that they would be able to step in someday when their help was needed, but for now, they helped by bracing the rickety metal folding chairs that served as makeshift ladders for the men lacing wires through the boughs. The *eyápaha* 'announcer' or 'emcee' oversaw the activities from his booth, testing the system from time to time by venturing comical criticism and commentary on the preparations.

Fewer people than expected filtered into the dance grounds where, for the first time in many years, the powwow was held at the same time as the Bennett County Fair and Rodeo. In the old days it was not uncommon to hold both events at the same time, but in more recent years the two events had been separated. The main local powwow was usually held at the Bear Creek *thiyóšpaye* just north of town. In fact, this year there was some contention from Bear Creek – some members of that community viewed a powwow in Martin in conjunction with the county fair and rodeo to be something of a compromise they were not willing to make. The timing of this event was also problematic because the shooting had occurred just eight months before, and homecoming was only one month away. People knew what had happened at the previous homecoming and had a good idea of what was to come. Events that might be viewed as conciliatory were not what the community needed, some thought.

This powwow had been planned by a recently retired Rosebud Lakota who was married to an Oglala woman. He is a World War II and Korean War veteran and had held jobs in Martin for many years. In fact, while officially retired, he still works part-time. He related to me that during the war, his commanding officer referred to him as "Chief," a term that pleased him since the officer placed great responsibility for reconnaissance in his hands. He saw the term as a compliment to his abilities and knew that his commanding officer recognized his skill in tracking through unknown territory. His vision for the future included peaceful relations among all segments of the Bennett County population, and this powwow was just one way for everyone to come together and have a good time. He was not blind to the problems in the community, but they did not form the center of his consciousness; he believed that to focus on problems while ignoring the positive aspects of community life would not be good for his grandchildren's generation. So, of course, a powwow was called for.

Blankets and lawn chairs with woven plastic seats were strewn about under the arbor, but there was an order to the chaos as one began to see familiar family groupings assemble. Women helped the youngsters adjust their dance outfits, and men also pitched in, teasing the younger ones. Lakota men seemed very comfortable caring for their children and were attentive to their needs. Teenagers in their dance outfits coyly flirted as they showed off their regalia, costly in terms of materials, but also in terms of time lovingly invested by family members who beaded complicated designs onto buckskin and embroidered dance shawls of wool or flowing polyester decorated with long fringe. The girls, many of whom I recognized from town, appeared transformed – they acted more shy, more feminine, in a Lakota way – in their lovely dance outfits. The boys seemed more confident out of their gangster chic, standing tall and proud in traditional dance outfits. They played easily with the younger ones who tried hard to emulate their elder siblings. Everyone had brought sandwiches or cookies or something else to eat while they waited for the powwow feast that would be provided by members of the organizer's family. Mostly, we all sat around watching the tiny tots practicing their dance steps and running around the center flagpole that bore the flags of the United States and the Oglala Sioux Tribe. I thought many of them to be too young to be able to walk but there they were, dancing.

The feast was about an hour late, drawing commentary from some of the elderly women who sat in lawn chairs under the arbor, but all was forgiven as the meal of baked ham, turkey, fried chicken, frybread, *wóžapi,* rolls, cakes, potato salad, *thaníǧa* 'tripe' soup, Jello, watermelon, and Kool-Aid commenced. Family members stood behind long tables and served over two hundred people, Indian and non-Indian alike. There was plenty to spare for liberal seconds. The monetary investment was considerable but more than worth the expense in terms of the honor that it brought to the generous family. In the summer, it was impossible to believe that anyone in this part of the country could go hungry – there were such feasts somewhere on the Pine Ridge or Rosebud reservations every weekend. The poor especially were encouraged to bring their own plastic containers and buckets to carry home abundant *wathéca* 'leftovers'. Such is the custom; the food preparers would rarely bring anything back home for themselves, serving as redistributors of community resources. I would often tease my Lakota grandmother about her "just being there for the food" (whether the venue was a powwow, a memorial, or the annual community dinner hosted by the local electric company) and not particularly caring about what was going on. As usual, she left this powwow loaded down with extra cans of coffee that had not been used as well as several shopping bags bulging with *wathéca*. She would be able to stretch her food stamps that month, and her children and grandchildren were once again the beneficiaries of a generous Lakota-style redistribution that has existed since prereservation times.

The grand entry procession was delayed a bit to enable its leader to make it back from his duties as Lakota representative and participant in the rodeo grand entry being held the equivalent of a city block away at the fairgrounds arena. He enjoyed doing double duty at community events because he loved to dance and display his Lakota style. He was an accomplished powwow dancer and a role model for children in the community – Lakota and non-Indian alike – who followed behind him, trying to pick up a few pointers. The year before, he had served as dance coach for the high school football player who played the role of Little Chief in the contested homecoming pageant. At last, the powwow commenced with the leader carrying a staff wrapped in fur, followed by a procession of dancers, mostly youngsters.

Lakota veterans of World War I, World War II, the Korean War, the Vietnam Conflict, and Operation Desert Storm marched with rifles to the Veterans' honor drum song. They fired their guns into the air, shattering the stillness, but many children who were used to this part of the powwow simply continued sleeping on their blankets under the arbor. Veterans wore red hawk feathers tied to their berets, an honor reserved for them, and many wore patches representing the American flag as well as the Oglala Lakota tribal flag sewn on their sleeves. Veterans were honored members of the community. A non-Indian man whispered to me that he wished "our boys" had received this kind of community support, which was often denied to U.S. soldiers after Vietnam. Support for military personnel is unflagging among Lakotas, not only because they ful-filled their responsibility to the United States government, but because veter-ans – warriors – were necessary for the continuity of the ceremonial elements of Lakota life. I recalled an earlier powwow at Pine Ridge that was organized to honor veterans, including a recent Congressional Medal of Honor recipient from the eastern part of the state. When I went to shake his hand, he was weep-ing. He said that even though he had lived his whole life in South Dakota, he had never visited a powwow until he had been invited to Pine Ridge as an hon-oree. He said that he wished that his own people had treated him as Pine Ridge treats its veterans. On the other hand, a few of the more vocal non-Indian Ben-nett County residents later commented that the Lakota practice of shooting guns during the Veterans' song had interrupted their enjoyment of the rodeo.

Although the number of dancers attending the three-day event did not meet the expectations of the organizers, they were impressed with the number of spectators. Many non-Indian tourists, some from as far away as Italy, Spain, and Germany, took pictures of the dancers. Some commented on one little dancer who wore an extraordinary outfit made of red sequins and beads. They won-dered why a little guy with striking blue eyes, red hair, and freckles was dancing in the powwow alongside his blond brother. They had not been in town long enough to recognize the family ties that confounded categorizations of people by racial characteristics. Those boys were recognized as Lakotas by their com-munity, and even more important, they were *dancers*.

After the rodeo, many more local non-Indians drifted in to see the pow-wow and ask about the significance of the various dance styles and regalia. The mood was easy. Lakotas were happy to answer respectful questions about pow-wows and the non-Indians, mostly gathered just outside the dance arbor, were content to observe from a slight distance.

I noticed a great number of local and tribal police officers patrolling the powwow grounds, but they were also relaxed, sharing jokes and conversation among themselves. There was no distance between the local sheriff and his deputies and tribal police officers, and they were obviously satisfied with the behavior of the crowd. When I asked them how they felt the celebration was going, they graced me with broad smiles. The community came together here as they watched the bright flashes of dancers circling around the flagpole that bore two symbolic representations of nationhood, flying together. Both were red, white, and blue and seemed to complement each other as they waved in the breeze.

After several hours of dance contests, a round dance was called for, allowing Lakotas and non-Indians alike to come together around the center pole. We joined hands, facing the center, and danced the round dance, which is simply

18. All colors touch the circle (Wild Horse Butte Powwow Parade float)

a shuffling step in time to the drumbeat. Many non-Indians chose, or were coerced, to dance. We commented that Lakotas were a tough people because, while the dance was simple enough, it worked leg, ankle, and foot muscles that we had not used in awhile. But when a sudden plains wind came up, we were forced to take cover. We dodged flying lawn chairs, paper plates and cups, and blinding dust, grabbed our belongings, and headed toward our cars.

It was an inauspicious ending to a community event enjoyed by all. We remarked that the wind likes to remind us who is really in charge in South Dakota.

THE COMBINED BENNETT COUNTY FAIR, RODEO, AND POWWOW PARADE

People again took their usual places on the shady side of Main Street, sitting on curbs or leaning against the storefronts. Kids readied themselves to dive for the candy that would be thrown from slow-moving vehicles. Knots of people chatted about the success of the powwow, rodeo, and fair. It was a community event with few outsiders except for some tourists, more difficult to identify today because many locals brought cameras as well. The parade formed in front of the Presbyterian church manse, as has long been the custom.

Veterans riding horses bore the flags of the United States and the Oglala

Sioux Tribe, as well as the blue and gold veterans' flag. They were followed by a man on a buckskin horse leading a riderless roan with a POW-MIA flag on the saddle. John Yellowbird Steele, the Oglala Sioux tribal chairman, walked behind. Young women riders carried the South Dakota state flag, followed by a float bearing flags representing local civic organizations and merchants. My Lakota sister rested her back against the whitewashed block wall of the Jack and Jill grocery store; her grandchild sneaked up and held up two fingers behind her head as I snapped her photo. Alice, the church dog, lay her head in Pastor Kate's lap contentedly and watched children dive for candy. A non-Indian man had set up his lawn chair near the curb. We could barely hear the speaker system a block away announce the entries, but we knew who they were without it.

Pickup trucks, surprisingly spiffed up and squeaky clean, had been transformed into mobile tableaux of historical Lakota life in contemporary context. Children and adult dancers rode along on hoods, roofs, and truck beds decorated with star quilts and dance shawls. Furred and feathered regalia drew gasps of approval from the crowd – they were beautiful, and the jingles, fashioned from Skoal and Copenhagen chewing tobacco lids formed into a cone shape and then sewn onto the dresses, shimmered in the sun against a cloudless and breathtakingly turquoise sky. There was a good turnout of dancers, especially since the powwow committee was giving points for attendance in the parade. Later, those points would be added to scores earned in the dance contests when determining prize money.

One float was entitled "Coming Together" and depicted four hands extended toward each other from the four cardinal directions. The hands were painted in the four Lakota colors – red, white, yellow, and black (frequently interpreted as the races of man) – and they met at a circle surrounding a cross, which looked like a medicine wheel, the emblem of the Oglala Sioux Tribe. A child dressed in a vivid red costume sat beneath the design, while her mother sat in a lawn chair cooling herself with a feather fan. The crowd showed its appreciation with extended applause.

Another float depicted a red hand and a white hand shaking in friendship, supported by a white frame in the shape of a tipi, under which stood a small Lakota girl. At the rear of the float stood a man in a traditional dance outfit, holding a fur-wrapped staff. Girls in street clothes tossed brightly wrapped candies to the scrambling tots.

The next contingent was led by a well-maintained stage coach drawn by two white horses. John Deere tractors pulled small floats representing local merchants and organizations. A high point was the horse-drawn buggy driven by the editors of the newspaper. The local woman who had sixty years before married that proud Nebraska farmboy rode in a place of honor, having that year been recognized as a Living Treasure by the South Dakota State Historical Society. Noisy fire trucks and the search and rescue vehicle painted bright yellow with impressive flames brought up the rear, as usual.

It was a good day for Bennett County. Fullblood, mixedblood, and white were, once again, distinct but unproblematic categories.

CONTEMPORARY SNAPSHOTS
IN THEIR HISTORICAL CONTEXT

My initial assessment of Bennett County, made on my first day at Geo's Cafe, was that identity here could be easily understood through a "neat structural analysis." I subsequently came to realize just how complicated individual, group, and regional identities really are here, especially when viewed at different times and through different lenses. Incidents surrounding the shooting of the local Lakota man provide an example of this. First, the federal government established a matrix of identity through its land policies, and federal legal and social categories established through policy still matter in contemporary community contexts. But, over time, this skeletal matrix acquired flesh and blood as arbitrary categories that were invested with meaning through social interactions, and complicated by the interpenetration and overlapping of various social fields. Those meanings are multivalent in the multiply coded social environment where everyone understands the potential valences. People maneuver by insisting on the multivalence of symbols and resist defining them. Karen Blu discusses Geertz's notion that "the sense of collective identity is to some extent 'unreflective', unselfconscious. Ideas about it need not always to be 'well-defined', nor need its symbols be unambiguous" (Blu 1980:231). Indeed, the power of polysemic markers of identity in Bennett County rests in their ambiguity and the ability of the local populations to mobilize certain identities in given situations unproblematically. Such strategies are effective because everyone understands their meanings. The meanings need not approximate those at the level of national discourse, but, rather, must suit the realities of life unique to Bennett County as a marginalized rural region that is defined by its distance from the core of state, national, and global politics.

The narrative snapshots presented in this study portray a community whose mood was in constant flux. The shooting occurred in mid December 1995, after a relatively stable period. That snapshot revealed a community in deep distress. Alcoholism, which is a problem in this region and is often a feature of poverty and social, psychic, or geographical isolation, was the catalyst for a rupture along racial faultlines. This rupture was compounded by outside forces that misinterpreted the tragic human incident in racial terms. Added to this was the fear of an unfriendly outside press that has repeatedly demonized Martin residents as irrepressible racists, outside pan-Indian groups with national political agendas that may be advanced at the expense of the local Lakotas who must continue to live in Martin after the headlines die down, and a potential economic boycott that would have injured the local Lakota consumers as much as the merchants. One high point was that *Indian Country Today*, a national weekly Indian newspaper, usually outspoken when it came to Martin, did not report the incident for three weeks. The editor, Tim Gaigo, who had been a resident of Martin for some time after moving his business from Pine Ridge to Martin before moving to Rapid City (see Nagel 1997:172), was acquainted with both the non-Indian rancher and the victim and properly identified the shooting as a consequence of alcohol abuse, labeling the incident an unfortunate community tragedy. The community sighed a collective sigh of relief, knowing the newspaper's national influence in Indian Country and recalling its role in demonizing Martin's residents for the homecoming debacle.

The victim's family's grief was marginalized and rendered invisible through the nonparticipation of the non-Indian community. The racialized atmosphere made it impossible for non-Indians to support the family in a public way. Non-Indian residents who fully understood that the shooting was related to alcohol were nonetheless unwilling to appear disloyal to one of their own – at least to the defendant's wife and family – by attending the wakes. In the same way, Lakotas who granted that the shooting was a tragic mistake still felt the need to comment that Bennett County justice might be lacking when it came to Indians. They were forced to ally themselves with the larger group, indicating that connection to a racial, ethnic, or cultural group often supercedes friendship in times when those differences are highlighted.

The success of the Wild Horse Butte Powwow held in conjunction with the Bennett County Fair and Rodeo in August 1996 can be attributed to one single factor. It was a celebration of diversity and pluralism in a small regional context. Non-Indians were not reinterpreting Lakota culture for Lakotas, and Lakotas were not reinterpreting ranching and farming culture for non-Indians. And more important, outsiders were not imposing values upon a community. The weekend was a celebration of pluralism and reflected a region that understood its history in its own way, and dealt with it on its own terms. People came together because they wanted to, rather than being driven to *pro forma* performances of identity in response to a divisive social crisis. No one was expected to choose sides, and each was allowed the privilege of participating in the powwow or rodeo as a human being, rather than as a representative of a larger social group that may or may not have been feuding with neighbors at the time.

A little over a month after the fair and powwow, social categories were invested with racial connotations once again. The high school homecoming was contested, with the help of outside political forces. Whether or not the Warrior symbol itself was offensive, many Lakota people were offended that it had been co-opted by the non-Indian community. There were other local Lakotas who did not really consider the issue to be worth fighting over but who were, nevertheless, forced to choose sides or else be marginalized by more vocal Indian community members and outsiders seeking a political forum. Either way, in this racialized circumstance, everyone's allegiance was suspect. Although the Warrior symbol was initially unproblematic, historical circumstances had changed and it will be difficult to depoliticize the symbol in the future. Bennett County is and will remain subject to political struggles outside of its social field.

UNINTENDED CONSEQUENCES:
WEAVING A REGION OF INSIDERS

Several common threads bind residents of Bennett County together in spite of their very different historical circumstances. All fear loss of their land and share a distrust of outsiders, especially so-called experts, federal agents with "new" policies, Indian activists with national reputations, their unsympathetic governor, and media vultures. Their fortunes and futures are woven together in a tenuous economic dependency on federal funds that are themselves unreliable due to the national politics of budget allocations. They all share the common experience of surviving here, and a deep love of the land that vexes them. Lakotas and their non-Indian neighbors in Bennett County have all experienced broken promises. The Dawes Act was intended to assimilate Lakotas into the dominant society by enabling them to pursue the American dream of owning private property. Shortly after the Dawes Act, and before the allotment process began on Pine Ridge Reservation, Lakotas were told that approximately one quarter of their remaining land base was deemed "surplus" and would be opened to accommodate homesteaders desiring to come to the plains. At the same time, homesteaders were told that in a mere twenty-five years they would have assimilated, taxpaying Lakota farmers as neighbors.

Fear of the loss of land – and precious identities rooted in it – underlie tensions between fullbloods, mixedbloods, and whites in Bennett County and underpin most public disputes between Lakotas and non-Indians. Comments such as "We are not going to give them one more inch" (mostly uttered by non-Indians), and "They stole our land" (spoken by Lakotas) are fighting words. Although contemporary local disputes concern relatively inconsequential issues (such as high school homecoming ceremonies, and whether or not to hold a powwow in conjunction with the county fair), undiluted anger, fear, and frustration remain just beneath the surface. Identities expressed in terms relating to

land and blood are constant reminders of a history of dispossession for Lakotas. Fear of a similar dispossession on the part of non-Indians whose land was
originally made available through the practice of forcing fee patents on "incompetent" Lakotas is also evident.

Amorphous federal policies built upon relationships to land and blood quantum as measures of competency and of identity have had consequences for all
county residents, but particularly for mixedbloods. On the one hand, mixedbloods were able to hold elected office and garner a certain amount of personal
power in the dominant U.S. system. On the other, they found themselves in
an ambiguous position that they could not control. On a personal level, the
case of mixedbloods exemplifies the limited success of federal policies designed
to assimilate Indians. While they had become "individuals" (Biolsi 1995), they
may also be viewed by some Indians, as well as non-Indians, as lacking a "real"
culture.

I learned something from my Indian and non-Indian students at Oglala
Lakota College when I assigned an essay on the topic of their life in Bennett County. Their essays consistently discussed non-Indian culture in societal
terms and Lakota culture in symbolic terms. Materialism is negatively valued
among Lakotas, being associated with a Euro-American, upwardly mobile,
grasping society based on a hierarchically arranged class structure. Lakota culture, on the other hand, is seen as based in language and traditional Lakota
values of generosity, acceptance of others incorporated into the tribe through
marriage or adoption, and distrust of political power as provisional, temporary, and situational. Conspicuous displays of wealth are still negatively perceived, while the correct performance of one's kinship role is highly valued.
The essays led me to consider how self-perception of Bennett County community members could depend upon worldview, and how different segments of
the community might view the scattered snapshots differently.

While there are three social categories of identity in Bennett County, fullblood, white, and mixedblood, there are only two cultural categories, Lakota
and Euro-American, and the two sets of categories are not easily reconciled.
Fullbloods fit unproblematically into the Lakota cultural category, characterized by those fullbloods as a culture based on spirituality, generosity, commu-
nitarianism, and humility. Facility in "the old language" as spoken by elderly
members of the tribe may also be a criterion in determining who is considered
a fullblood. Fullbloods are generally understood to be "treaty Indians" who do
not accept the notion of tribal government based on the United States model,
and who still argue that changes based on that model have led to a hierarchical arrangement that does not serve all segments of the Pine Ridge population equitably. For the most part, fullbloods continue Lakota cultural practices,

even though many are also Christians who attend mission churches scattered throughout the reservation. Many fullbloods are poor by Euro-American standards, but those who live on their own allotments are considered fortunate, despite living conditions that might be considered substandard by city dwellers. Fullbloods who are landless and live in Martin or in HUD cluster housing are considered truly pitiful; they are often victims of crime and rely more on the federal government than on family connections in other districts, perhaps because of unreliable access to transportation and telephone service.

Non-Indians, likewise, fit unproblematically into a Euro-American cultural category, characterized by individualism, strong work ethic, materialism, upward mobility, dominance, and power. They are associated with materialistic accumulation of wealth and, often, conspicuous displays of social status in their choices of homes, clothing, and vehicles.

More complicated is the case of mixedbloods, who do not fit neatly into either cultural category and can move between them according to the context. For the most part, mixedbloods value American ideals of self-improvement and upward mobility, and have often received a better formal education than fullbloods. Such advances leave them in an ambivalent position. They are often looked down upon by fullbloods, who see them as having "bought into the white world," becoming "stuck-up and selfish," and failing to maintain their kinship obligation of generosity with extended family relations. I have heard the process of "moving up in the world" expressed in terms of a "bucket of worms" or a "bucket of crabs." Having finally reached the lip of the bucket (after crawling over the backs of relatives to get there), the aspiring one is dragged back down again into the "mire" of the kinship system. Those dynamics make for difficult relationships between mixedbloods and their fullblood relatives, driving wedges between those conceptual categories of people.

Non-Indians resent the fact that their mixedblood kin are entitled, by virtue of having at least one quarter Lakota blood, to membership in the tribe and the accompanying economic benefits. Affirmative action policies enable Indian-owned businesses to receive first consideration in contracts with the tribe as well as with state and federal entities. The free health, dental, and vision services that mixedbloods receive infuriate many whites because they must pay for – and often drive long distances for – services that may be inferior to those received by Indians. While Indians may be admitted to the county hospital for emergency services, no such provision for non-Indians exists in the Indian Health Service. In one instance, after consuming a monstrously large cinnamon roll at the famous Big Bat's Texaco station in Pine Ridge, I was forced to call the local tribal hospital to ask if it would be possible to buy some insulin and a needle since I had forgotten to take my insulin and had left it at home. I was told to drive the sixty miles back to Martin to get it. When I asked if there were any circumstance in which I *could* receive a shot, I was told, "Yeah, if you fall into a coma and are brought here."

Mixedbloods often qualify for certain educational opportunities, whereas whites do not. Many scholarships intended for Indian children are given to mixedblood children who have experienced a culturally white upbringing by parents who emphasized good study habits. Indian and white parents alike complain that such scholarships were intended for poor fullbloods, and that wealthy mixedbloods should not be allowed to capitalize on opportunities meant for people who need them more. The arguments between whites and fullbloods are not nearly as vociferous as those between whites or fullbloods against mixedbloods.

Rather than being able to claim either cultural identity at all times and in all contexts, mixedbloods may instead have a particular range of potentialities, a situational ethnicity, if you will. They are often defined as standing in "opposition to" rather than as "a member of," and are perceived locally as "in-betweens," or "hyphenated" people.

But if we pan back from individual and local negotiations of identity, we find a region that has its own unique identity formed through political marginalization and geographical isolation. Its problems of internal boundary maintenance pale in the face of outside national processes that continue to stir the pot, hearkening back to Ella C. Deloria's prophetic words:

> And it came, and without their asking for it – a totally different way of life, far-reaching in its influence, awful in its power, insistent in its demands. It came like a flood that nothing could stay. . . . and [gave] them but one choice – to conform to it, or else! And this it could force them to do because, by its very presence, it was even then making their way no longer feasible. [Deloria 1944:76–77]

This time, it is technological advances that are making it nearly impossible for family-oriented farmers and ranchers to compete with agribusiness and commercial feedlots. The irony is not lost on the descendants of early Bennett County settlers, some of whom find that they must hold low-paying service jobs in Martin in order to keep their land. They understand that the rhetoric of removal that had once been directed solely toward Lakotas now also applies to their circumstances. They realize that early attacks on Lakota tradition as being hide-bound and maladaptive for the early twentieth century are similar to contemporary economic attacks on traditional rural life at the turn of the twenty-first. They find that their own governor cannot be considered an ally.

19. Fullblood? Mixedblood? White? All we know is that they dance!

Identity politics are the least of their troubles, but they do feel some sense of control in that area, so the dance continues.

Bennett County was one of the last places in the continental United States to be intentionally settled through actions directly related to federal policies, and the distance between the "established and the outsider" (Elias and Scotson 1994; Dominy 1995) was not so clearly defined from the outset. Longstanding kinship ties among Lakotas (DeMallie 1979:221–41, 1994) that preceded their resettlement were actively manipulated by early white traders and settlers to assure some measure of social and economic security. Those alliances allowed non-Indian men who married into Lakota families to acquire land by taking advantage of federal policies that professed to guarantee a land base, annuities, and health care to Lakotas.

In twenty-first-century Bennett County, stresses arise when residents are confronted with unpleasant historical realities beyond their control that require a conceptual move away from mythical past to ambivalent present. The myth of the frontier – of noble savages and fiercely independent white settlers – is easy for most of us to imagine because it is constantly reinforced through representations in American popular culture. When those images are contextualized by anthropologists and historians, the contemporary moral order is put at risk. The precarious social equilibrium that exists in Bennett County is a consequence of, above all else, shifting federal policies concerning property relations. Each group's ancestors were settled here either by federal mandate, as in the case of the Lakotas, or invitation, as in the case of early homesteaders, and each group depends on federal subsidies that bolster an inviable economy. These groups have more in common than they may wish to see, and the history of the region discloses less frontier independence than they care to admit. And if you look carefully, and from a particularly focused point of view that includes both the everyday and the extraordinary, you will see insiders dancing together. Some of them are more familiar with powwow dancing, while others are more at home with the two-step, but sometimes they change partners for an intimate regional dance – at arms length – on the plains of South Dakota. Masters of intimacy and avoidance, they dance it well.

Traditions in the Making, 1997

I put off leaving Bennett County so that I could spend my last night in town at the opening of the second annual Wild Horse Butte Powwow. There were many more dancers this year, many of whom had danced a couple of weeks previously at the Bear Creek powwow. More non-Indian community members also attended and the mood was one of excitement, since this event seemed to be catching on. The scene was very much the same as it had been the year before except that the powwow was now established, with a history, albeit brief, for attendees to comment upon. It was continuity in the making, and already those of us who had attended the first powwow could comment on the fact that this was a great improvement over last year. More people danced, more Indian tacos were sold, and there were more booths selling powwow tapes, dream catchers, beadwork, and other jewelry. I visited under the dance arbor with the elderly woman from Wanblee who had spoken against the homecoming ceremony at the AIM march the year before. This year she was back to watch with delight as her grandchildren danced, and to catch up on Bennett County gossip.

About a month later, a friend sent me a videotape of the 1997 Bennett County Warrior homecoming. I had heard that the students were finally able to get the tradition changed so that they could get back to being kids and not pass the discord down to their younger siblings. The students were ready for a change, and a change it was. The American Legion Memorial Auditorium was only half full of well-wishers as the princess candidates lined up for their moments in the limelight. The buckskin dresses had been replaced by street clothes that were neither casual nor fancy. Princess candidates wore identical simple blue sleeveless shifts cut to mid thigh, and high heels. Their escorts wore freshly pressed white shirts and thin ties as they waited their turn to lead the candidates toward the stage. There was no solemn drumbeat. Instead, in line with the 1997 homecoming "Rock-and-Roll" theme, the sounds of "Hippy Hippy Shake," "Wooly

Bully," and "Do You Believe In Magic?" blasted out of the speakers. Instead of a tipi, stars, and campfire, the stage was decorated with large representations of phonograph records. Even the purple and gold banner that used to hang in front of the stage had been removed for the occasion – the word "Warrior" was not in evidence. Still, the cheerleaders who opened the show shouted a "Go Warriors!" cheer, which was well received by the small audience.

The event was very much like a pep rally, with commentary from the coaches and cheers from the crowd. A series of skits was planned, and the seventh graders began with the theme "Wipeout," depicting the opposing team in decrepit condition at halftime after being brutalized by the Bennett County football team. That skit was followed by "Footloose," in which girls gave their interpretations of 1970s and 1980s dances, such as the Frug, the Monkey, and the Twist. Their dances conveyed the appropriate mood of controlled chaos. This was followed by football players in drag, dancing to the tune of "It's In His Kiss"; a skit called "Yellow Submarine"; and a skit performed by the faculty, who sang "I Wish I Were a Bennett County Warrior" to the tune of a highly recognizable hot dog commercial jingle. It seemed from the video that a good time was had by all, although a brief sentence in the local newspaper noted that, despite all the changes and concessions to the demands of last year's protestors, none of those protestors showed up to witness the modified event.

THINGS CHANGE:
BENNETT COUNTY REVISITED, 2001

Crossing the Pine Ridge Reservation border in June, 2001, after having dropped down from Wyoming on Highway 18 from the north and west, I mused that I would be reversing my original entry to Bennett County. It had been two years since my last visit and seven years since my first.

The land was muted in the pre-storm atmosphere, sweetclover that had pioneered along the highways swaying delicately as I pulled into the Prarie Wind Casino to wager a few bucks on the Stampede dollar slot machine. It had become a place of pilgrimage for me, a place where I didn't mind "contributing" a bit to the Oglala Sioux Tribe. I noted the license plates on tour buses from as far away as Minnesota and observed that business was pretty good for a Monday morning and that more whites than Indians were feeding the machines. The place was hopping!

After an hour or two I headed on to my next usual stop, the Holy Rosary Mission, to visit with Brother Simon and to see the Red Cloud Art Show that features the work of up and coming Native American artists. My favorite this year was a large painting that was simple but striking in its primary colors. It read, "One drop of Indian blood . . . a tub of white lard." Another painted on ledger paper depicted a trickster figure sneaking off with a ballot, entitled "Chad," an obvious allusion to the 2000 presidential election. The humorous entries always attracted me because they so fully reflect that deadly Indian sense of humor. Only those who see situations clearly can comment in utterly irreverent ways. Holy Rosary is one of my favorite places to catch up on local gossip and hear about the people I know who have been passing through.

In Pine Ridge Village I resisted seeing what Big Bat's Texaco looked like now that they are rebuilding after a destructive fire. I will miss the pink and purple neon signs pointing out the ATM and those monstrous cinnamon buns that cause diabetics such delight and pain.

I drove the speed limit – just barely – rubbernecking like a nosy neighbor at things remembered and unremembered that stood atop the land. But the land and the sky were what I remembered most, and they caused me to relax into the seat, be content with the speed limit, and just sense that they were welcoming me back to a place that I have long considered to be a home away from home.

I did not take the road to Wounded Knee where I usually sit pondering man's inhumanity to man and the resilience of the souls in South Dakota while smoking a cigarette down to the filter on the always windy hill. I don't recall learning to scatter a little tobacco there at the mass grave, but I always did. I would come back in a couple of days when my mind was more relaxed and when I was satisfied that I had seen the Martin watertower that had been painted sky blue, but never really matched the perfect color of the sky.

Batesland passed, and then Swett, and the Allen turnoff where a new package liquor store and bar stuck out like a sore thumb. I slammed on the brakes as someone in the car ahead decided to make an unsignaled turn into the driveway.

Finally I saw the cluster of trees that marked that wide spot in the road. It seemed a little wider than when I had first encountered it, but it was still a small island of trees anchored tenuously to the plains.

It had changed. Some merchants had folded their tents, and others had come. A combination museum and city office building was brand new and due to open on the Fourth of July. The *Booster II* had a young new editor with a fresher outlook, housing units had sprung up in clusters like daffodils, and there was yet another new sheriff, with a new bride, the 1996 Warrior Princess. There was a real stoplight in town next to the Amoco that was once a Standard station. Bennett County High School Warrior homecomings had boasted original, student-selected themes, including a salute to Hawai'i complete with grass skirts, bare feet, and leis. The Markota Restaurant was now the Dakota, and Geo's on Main Street is now under Lakota ownership and management. The once-deserted Ace hardware store has been replaced by a "$ Store," and Justus Video now occupies the defunct Western wear store, but the Martin Mercantile, Triple Z, Jack and Jill's, and the Country Market remain with friendly faces from the past. Billionaire Ted Turner bought 37,664 acres southwest of Martin for $200 per acre, and there are other wealthy absentee landlords who have bought land that they are not using, or perhaps will turn into buffalo grazing land. I wonder what John Locke would have thought of the recolonization of the West by wealthy outsiders who do not "improve" the land or participate as neighbors in local affairs. Maybe we can claim a piece, if we promise to "improve" it?

Demographics are changing as well. In Martin, the 2000 U.S. Census reveals that of a city population of 1,106, there are 597 non-Indians, 416 Indians, 7 African-Americans, and 1 Asian. There is no category for mixedblood. Indian children represent approximately seventy percent of the elementary school population, sixty percent of the junior high school, and in the kindergarten class, of forty-eight total, thirty-eight are Lakota, nine are non-Indian, and one is African-American (Belinda Ready, p.c. 2001).

While some people have died, others have moved on; even the South Dakota Living Treasure and her non-Indian husband are now Texans. Many familiar faces are still here, and images of the past are ingrained in family memories and stories retold at family and community gatherings. Overlapping histories may conflict, but they make up the moral core of the region and sustain it. These stories are what makes this place unique and a counterpoint to places in which conflicts as described in these narrative snapshots go unmentioned, or become perhaps only a brief footnote in daily affairs because they are so frequent as to be a ubiquitous and grating background hum.

Even here, time does not stand still. For that, I am glad to have my narrative scrapbook that spans from 1995–97 to look back on to recall the Bennett County that I observed. Will the potential for community crises remain? Undoubtedly. The potential for heroism? Most certainly. And neighborly relations? Perhaps. Will the prairie remain the core of the community? Of course – she is its heart.

NOTES

CHAPTER 1

1. In 1990, apparently for reasons of space, Rand McNally and Company omitted North Dakota, South Dakota, and Oklahoma from its United States travel atlas. According to Anne Matthews, "the editor explained blithely that Plains states seemed least likely to be missed" (1992:55). Linda Hasselstrom writes that "a large part of the rest of the world thinks our state [South Dakota] is nearly worthless, an arid expanse fit for garbage and exploitation and nothing else," and that when Rand McNally noticed the omission, a spokesperson explained that "no one would want to come here" (1991:xix).

2. Throughout this study, there will be many terms relating to American Indians, both in local contexts and in more general contexts, such as federal documents. The American Indians addressed in this study are primarily Oglala Lakotas living in Bennett County, South Dakota and on the Pine Ridge Indian Reservation. The local term for Lakotas is often simply "Indian."

3. As early as 1936, the U.S. government recognized the fragility of the Great Plains region and recommended that prevailing attitudes be acknowledged and addressed so that the plains could continue to flourish. The document enumerated attitudes of Western thinking in need of revision: that man conquers nature; that natural resources are inexhaustible; that habitual practices are the best; that what is good for the individual is good for everybody; that a property owner may do as he likes with the property; that markets will continue to expand indefinitely; that free competition coordinates industry and agriculture; that values will increase indefinitely; that tenancy is a stepping-stone to ownership; that the factory farm is generally desireable; that the individual must make his own adjustments. These "attitudes of mind" have only strengthened over the six and a half decades since the report. See U.S. Government (1936:63–67).

4. Given the federal price supports that influence and aid ranching and agriculture in this region, the notion of "The Market" seems inappropriate. See, for example, U.S. Government (1936:65).

5. I would like to thank Christina Burke for conversations that led to identifying the camera as a useful metaphor.

CHAPTER 2

1. See Nagel (1997) for a comprehensive discussion of the American Indian Movement, and Matthiessen's (1991) discussion of Leonard Peltier.

2. Much of the discussion in this section appeared in Wagoner (1998a).

3. The original six districts of Pine Ridge were White Clay, Wakpamni, Porcupine, Wounded Knee, Medicine Root, and Pass Creek. Bennett County was once included in the Pass Creek district, but the boundaries subsequently changed, and Eagle Nest and LaCreek districts were added. Bennett County is now in the LaCreek district (One Feather 1974).

4. Letter from John Brennan to Hon. E.W. Martin, Washington, D.C. Feb. 1, 1909. Brennan Family Papers (H72.2) Letterbook 1906. South Dakota State Historical Resource Center, Pierre.

5. Proceedings of Council held by James McLaughlin, Inspector, with the Indians of Pine Ridge, South Dakota, with reference to opening the south-eastern portion of Pine Ridge Reservation, as contemplated by Senate Bill No. 2341, 61st Congress, 1st Session. Sept. 1, 1909. Brennan Family Papers.

6. Ibid.

7. Ibid.

8. Ibid.

9. The Bennett County Historical Association's account states that the meeting was held in "about 1910" in Allen, and that "there was a 100 per cent vote in favor of the proposition." However, according to the minutes of the meeting, which was actually held on September 15, 1909, that assessment is far from correct.

10. Proceedings of Council, Sept. 9, 1909. Brennan Family Papers.

11. Ibid.

12. Ibid.

13. Ibid.

14. Ibid.

15. Of the 762,698 acres, 548,229 were held in deeded status, and 198,442 were held in tribal trust status. A 1935 Executive Order set aside 16,027 acres for the Lacreek National Wildlife Refuge. See Bennett County Historical Society (1981:63).

16. For a delightful collection of life histories of the early Lakota and non-Indian settlers in Allen, South Dakota, see Lewis 1980. This volume is important because it relates stories of everyday life that are not "political." In addition, several family histories have been compiled by Bennett County residents. See, for example, Jacobs (1985, 1996), Long (1975), Fanning (1994), and Bennett County Retired Teachers' Association (1986, 1988).

CHAPTER 3

1. Figures and statistics were provided by the Bennett County Assessor in November 1997.

2. The Wheeler-Howard Act, June 18, 1934, referred to as the Indian Reorganization Act (IRA), will not be specifically dealt with here; however, it had widespread implications for American Indian tribes, including conserving and developing resources on Indian land, the right to form businesses and other organizations, establishing a credit system, granting certain rights self-rule, and providing vocational education. See text in Prucha (1990:222–25) and discussion in Prucha (1984:954–68, 993–1005). For Franklin Roosevelt's views on the bill, see Cohen (1971:xix). For an overview of twentieth-century federal Indian policies, see Washburn (1971:75–139). See also Biolsi (1992) for a thorough discussion of the effects of the IRA on the neighboring Rosebud Reservation. Many of his examples apply to Pine Ridge as well.

3. One mixedblood Lakota from Bennett County, now the president of a tribal college in Montana, related to me his fears for both Indian and non-Indian education in rural areas. He noted that education is often geared toward skills not needed in ranching or farming areas. He also noted that more non-Indian students ultimately leave rural areas to find jobs than Indian graduates, who were, in his words, "more connected to family and land." Non-Indians also felt that the result of education was the removal of people from rural areas.

4. Brennan's 1910 annual report reflects underemployment among fullbloods, as well as a disadvantage in the total capital invested in business: fullbloods – $3000; mixedbloods – $10,000; whites – $60,000 (Superintendent's Annual Narrative and Statistical Report. August 10, 1910. BIA 1907–38. M1011, Roll 106).

5. For a discussion of the different ethnic groups immigrating to and emigrating from western South Dakota, see Nelson (1986). A "pecking order" still exists in Bennett County, with descendants of French, Swiss, and other western European stock considered to be of a higher status than descendants of eastern Europeans. This is often evidenced in joking behaviors.

6. Only recently have relationships between biogenetically unrelated members of the same sex been a subject of battles for legal recognition, hence these do not apply to this argument concerning the imposition of foreign categories of relationship on nineteenth-century Lakotas.

7. Locke's values were naturally the product of philosophies that preceded him. For an enlightening discussion of the evolution of Lockean thinking, see Williams (1990).

8. On October 22, 1995, Means, who was promoting his new book, *Where White Men Fear to Tread*, was interviewed by Leanne Hanson on National Public Radio's "Weekend Edition." Means said, "I really always wanted to be an Indian . . . and when the American Indian Movement came along, that afforded me the opportunity." This interview occurred a little more than two months before the shooting (quoted in Nagel 1997, n. 35:181).

CHAPTER 4

1. Much of this chapter is based on Wagoner (1997).

2. The federal government distinguished major crimes in Indian Country from minor ones in the Major Crimes Act of 1885 (Prucha 1990:167–68). The law was enacted after *Ex Parte Crow Dog* (1883), in which federal courts ruled that the Rosebud Sioux Tribe had jurisdiction over a case involving the murder of one Indian by another. (See Harring 1994 for an excellent discussion of the case and its implications for tribal autonomy.) Not satisfied with the sentence imposed by the tribe, Congress moved to extend federal jurisdiction over certain serious crimes in Indian Country. The original seven crimes were extended to fourteen and include murder, manslaughter, kidnapping, maiming, felonious sexual molestation of a minor, incest, assault with intent to commit murder, assault with a dangerous weapon, assault resulting in serious bodily injury, arson, burglary, and robbery (see Canby 1988:132–35). This was a major encroachment by federal authority on reservation affairs. (For a portion of the Major Crimes Act, as well as a portion of the Indian Crimes Act of 1976, see Prucha 1990:167–68, 278. See also Washburn 1971:170–71; Prucha 1984:678–79.)

3. Pine Ridge is included in Fall River County for administrative purposes. Shortly after Bennett County seceded from Pine Ridge Reservation, it also broke its ties to Fall River. Bennett County residents wanted their taxes to be used closer to home, fearing that Fall River would not return a fair share of revenues collected here for necessary services. As a result, when the tribe needs a county sheriff to enter their reservation to deal with minor non-Indian violations, Fall River authorities are contacted.

4. Certain exceptions to this rule apply. Alaska Natives, Oklahoma tribes, Hawaiian Natives, New York Indians, California Indians, and Terminated tribes are considered "Special Groups" (Cohen 1982:739–818).

5. See DeMallie (1980) for an excellent illustration of the difficulty that representatives of fundamentally different cultures encountered in communicating important abstract concepts during the treaty era.

6. See Lazarus (1991) for a discussion of litigation against the U.S. government by the Sioux Nation based on withholding of rations that led some Sioux individuals to sign away their claim to the Black Hills and other lands. A reexamination of the case by the U.S. Supreme Court led to the decision to grant the Sioux tribes a sizeable cash settlement. Fearing that accepting any payment for the government's illegal seizure of the Black Hills would imply that they gave up their right to the land, the Sioux refused to accept the settlement. The money remains in the bank, gathering interest.

7. For much greater detail on the Dawes Act, see D.S. Otis (1973 [1934]); Cohen (1982 ed.:129–143); Clinton et al. (1991:147–152); Hoxie (1984); Prucha (1984:658–896). For text of the Dawes Act, see Prucha (1990:171–74).

8. During the allotment era, "Indian-held lands [in the continental U.S.] declined from 138 million acres in 1887 to 48 million in 1934, 20 million of which was desert" (Holt and Forrester 1990:5).

9. For a thorough discussion of forced fee patents and Competency Commission practices, see McDonnell (1991:90–104, 1989:21–34).

10. Mr. Long has allowed me to use his name because his appraisal of jurisdictional disputes and the problems that he believes to have been created by the federal government have been stated in lectures and in print.

11. Mr. Long was referring to states that do not fall under Public Law 280 (Prucha 1990:233–34). The law enables states enacting it to extend state jurisdiction over offenses committed by or against Indians in certain areas of Indian Country. PL 280 states include Alaska, California, Minnesota, Nebraska, Oregon, and Wisconsin. See Clinton et al. (1991:594–622) for a full discussion of this complicated law and the reasons why some states with large Indian populations did not enact it.

12. Mr. Long was referring to an earlier conversation with Thomas Biolsi, and fully attributes both the concept and the quotation to him. See Getches and Wilkinson (1986: 42–110) for an intensive discussion of the formative years of Indian law. The case cited here is *Worcester v Georgia* (Prucha 1990:60–62).

13. Several of the consultants cited in this section have left Bennett County since our initial interviews. The data presented here were culled from interviews given while they still worked in the county.

14. It is not difficult to understand why people are confused about the actual status of Bennett County in relation to Pine Ridge. Maps supplied by the Aberdeen office of the Bureau of Indian Affairs include Bennett County as part of the reservation. A map included in a 1996 document distributed by the U.S. Department of Commerce also does not differentiate between Bennett County and Pine Ridge Indian Reservation (see Tiller 1996:555, 560–61). Note that map 1 distinguishes Bennett County by including Shannon and Washabaugh (now named Jackson) counties within Pine Ridge Reservation.

15. Local residents who carry vehicle insurance must pay exorbitant rates for collision coverage to guarantee recovery of damages incurred from accidents involving the many unlicensed and uninsured drivers on local roads.

16. See Cohen (1982:300–304) for a detailed discussion of the Major Crimes Act.

17. See *Cook v Parkinson*, 525 Fed. 2d 120 (8th Cir. 1975), and *Rosebud Sioux Tribe v Kneipp*, 430 US 584, 51 L Ed 2d 660, 97 S Ct 1361.

18. The court held that suits under the Indian Civil Rights Act were barred because of the sovereign immunity of tribes and that the proper place for dealing with these disputes was in tribal court (Holt and Forrester 1990:27).

19. Biolsi (1995) earlier made reference to the negative racial dynamics inherent in checkerboard jurisdiction.

20. On January 15, 1987 (ironically, one hundred years after the adoption of the Dawes Act), the court unanimously held that the claims were barred by the statute of limitations and therefore could not be litigated.

REFERENCES

Abourezk, James G.

    1989 Advise and Dissent: Memoirs of South Dakota and the U.S. Senate. Chicago: Lawrence Hill Books.

Ambrose, Stephen E.

    1975 Crazy Horse and Custer: The Parallel Lives of Two American Warriors. Garden City, N.Y.: Doubleday.

Anderson, Harry H.

    1973 Fur Traders as Fathers: The Origins of the Mixed-Blooded Community among Rosebud Sioux. South Dakota History 3:233–70.

Basso, Keith H.

    1996 Wisdom Sits in Places: Notes on Western Apache Landscape. *In* Senses of Place, edited by Steven Feld and Keith H. Basso, 53–90. Santa Fe: School of American Research Press.

Baudrillard, Jean

    1989 America. New York: Verso.

Baumgartner, M. P.

    1988 The Moral Order of a Suburb. New York: Oxford University Press.

Bennett County Historical Society

    1981 70 Years of Pioneer Life in Bennett County South Dakota 1911–1981. Pierre: State Publishing Co.

Bennett County Retired Teachers' Association

    1988 Bennett County Brands – Gems of the Past, 1889–1989. 2d ed. Unpublished manuscript in author's possession.

Bennett, John W.

    1969 Northern Plainsmen: Adaptive Strategy and Agrarian Life. Arlington Heights, Ill.: AHM.

Bennett, John W., and Seena B. Kohl

    1995 Settling the Canadian-American West, 1890–1915: Pioneer Adaptation and Community Building. Lincoln: University of Nebraska Press.

Berkhofer, Robert F.

    1978 The White Man's Indian: Images of the American Indian, Columbus to the Present. New York: Knopf.

Biolsi, Thomas

    1992 Organizing the Lakota: The Political Economy of the New Deal on the Pine Ridge and Rosebud Reservations. Tucson: University of Arizona Press.

    1995 The Birth of the Reservation: Making the Modern Individual among the Lakota. American Ethnologist 22:28–53.

Blinderman, A.

    1978 Congressional Social Darwinism and the American Indian. The Indian Historian 11(2):15–17.

Blu, Karen I.

    1980 The Lumbee Problem: The Making of an American Indian People. Cambridge: Cambridge University Press.

    1996 "Where Do You Stay At?": Homeplace and Community among the Lumbee. In Senses of Place, edited by Steven Feld and Keith H. Basso, 197–227. Santa Fe: School of American Research Press.

Braroe, Neils Winthur

    1975 Indian and White: Self-Image and Interaction in a Canadian Plains Community. Stanford, Calif.: Stanford University Press.

Butler, Anne M.

    1994 Selling the Popular Myth. In The Oxford History of the American West, edited by Clyde A. Milner II et al., 771–801. New York: Oxford University Press.

Canby, William C., Jr.

    1988 American Indian Law in a Nutshell. 2d ed. (Nutshell Series.) St. Paul, Minn.: West Publishing Co.

Carlson, Leonard A.

    1981 Indians, Bureaucrats, and Land. Westport, Conn.: Greenwood Press.

Child, Brenda J.

    1998 Boarding School Seasons. Lincoln: University of Nebraska Press.

Churchill, Ward, and James Vander Wall

    1988 Agents of Repression: The FBI's Secret Wars against the Black Panther Party and the American Indian Movement. Boston: South End Press.

Clinton, Hillary

    1996 It Takes a Village: And Other Lessons Children Teach Us. New York: Simon and Schuster.

Clinton, Robert N., Nell Jessup Newton, and Monroe E. Price.

    1991 American Indian Law. 3d ed. (Contemporary Legal Education Series.) Charlottesville, Va.: The Michie Company.

Clow, Richmond

   1981 A Report on The Bureau of Indian Affairs Fee Patenting and Canceling
   Policies, 1900–1942. Prepared for the Aberdeen Area Office Rights Protection
   Branch in Compliance with the Bureau of Indian Affairs 2415 Claims Program.
   Copy on file in Oglala Lakota College Archives, Kyle, South Dakota.

Cohen, Felix S.

   1971 Handbook of Federal Indian Law. Albuquerque: University of New
   Mexico Press.

   1982 Felix S. Cohen's Handbook of Federal Indian Law. 2d ed. Edited by
   Charles F. Wilkinson. Charlottesville, Va.: The Michie Company.

Comaroff, Jean

   1985 Body of Power, Spirit of Resistance: The Culture and History of a South
   African People. Chicago: University of Chicago Press.

Comaroff, John, and Jean Comaroff

   1992 Ethnography and the Historical Imagination. Boulder, Colo.: Westview
   Press.

Cronon, William

   1983 Changes in the Land: Indians, Colonists, and the Ecology of New
   England. New York: Hill and Wang.

Daniels, Robert E.

   1970 Cultural Identities among the Oglala Sioux. In The Modern Sioux: Social
   Systems and Reservation Culture, edited by Ethel Nurge, 198–245. Lincoln:
   University of Nebraska Press.

Debo, Angie

   1986 A History of the Indians of the United States. Norman: University of
   Oklahoma Press.

Deloria, Ella C.

   1944 Speaking of Indians. New York: Friendship Press. Reprint, 1998, Lincoln: University of Nebraska Press.

Deloria, Philip J.

   1998 Playing Indian. New Haven, Conn.: Yale University Press.

Deloria, Vine, Jr.

   1970 We Talk, You Listen: New Tribes, New Turf. New York: Macmillan.

Deloria, Vine, Jr., and Raymond J. DeMallie, eds.

   1999 Documents of American Indian Diplomacy: Treatys, Agreements, and
   Conventions, 1775–1979. 2 vols. Norman: University of Oklahoma Press.

Deloria, Vine Jr., and Clifford Lytle

   1984 The Nations Within: The Past and Future of American Indian Sovereignty. New York: Pantheon Books.

DeMallie, Raymond J.

   1978 Pine Ridge Economy: Cultural and Historical Perspectives. In American Indian Economic Development, edited by Sam Stanley, 243. The Hague: Mouton.

1979 Change in American Indian Kinship Systems: The Dakota. *In* Currents in Anthropology: Essays in Honor of Sol Tax, edited by Robert Hinshaw, 221–41.The Hague: Mouton.

1980 Touching the Pen: Plains Indian Treaty Councils in Ethnohistorical Perspective. *In* Ethnicity on the Great Plains, edited by Frederick C. Luebke, 38–53. Lincoln: University of Nebraska Press.

1994 Kinship and Biology in Sioux Culture. *In* Anthropology of North American Indians: Essays in Culture and Social Organization, edited by Raymond J. DeMallie and Alfonso Ortiz, 125–46. Norman: University of Oklahoma Press.

Dewing, Rolland
>   1985 Wounded Knee: The Meaning and Significance of the Second Incident. New York: Irvington Press.

Dominy, Michèle D.
>   1995 White Settler Assertions of Native Status. American Ethnologist 22:358–74.

Elias, Norbert, and John L. Scotson
>   1994 The Established and the Outsiders: A Sociological Enquiry into Community Problems. 2d ed. Thousand Oaks, Calif.: Sage Publications.

Fanning, Jerry
>   1994 Through the Raspberry Patch: An Autobiography of the Earlier Years. Unpublished manuscript in author's possession.

Feld, Steven, and Keith H. Basso, eds.
>   1996 Senses of Place. Santa Fe: School of American Research Press.

Feraca, Stephen E., and Howard, James H.
>   1963 The Identity and Demography of the Dakota or Sioux Tribe. Plains Anthropologist, 7(20):80–84.

Fite, Gilbert C.
>   1985 "The Only Thing Worth Working For": Land and Its Meaning for Pioneer Dakotans. South Dakota History 15:2–25.

Fogelson, Raymond D.
>   1998 Perspectives on Native American Identity. *In* Studying Native America, edited by Russell Thornton, 40–59. Madison: University of Wisconsin Press.

Furber, Bradley B.
>   1991 Two Promises, Two Propositions: The Wheeler-Howard Act as a Reconciliation of the Indian Law Civil War. University of Puget Sound Law Review 14:211–82.

Gay, Robert
>   1984 The Crook(ed) Commission of 1889 at Pine Ridge. Unpublished manuscript in Oglala Lakota College Archives

1985 Theft of Bennett County. Paper prepared for the Nineteenth Dakota History Conference. Unpublished manuscript in Oglala Lakota College Archives.

Geertz, Clifford

1983 Local Knowledge. New York: Basic Books.

1996 Afterword. *In* Senses of Place, edited by Steven Feld and Keith H. Basso, 259–62. Santa Fe: School of American Research Press.

Getches, David H., and Charles F. Wilkinson, eds.

1986 Federal Indian Law: Cases and Materials. 2d ed. St. Paul, Minn.: West Publishing Company.

Gordon, Robert J.

1992 The Bushman Myth: The Making of a Namibian Underclass. Boulder, Colo.: Westview Press.

Greenhouse, Carol J.

1986 Praying for Justice: Faith, Order, and Community in an American Town. Ithaca: Cornell University Press.

Hall, Philip S.

1991 To Have This Land. Vermillion: University of South Dakota Press.

Hansen, Sandra

1991 Survey of Civil Jurisdiction in Indian Country 1990. *In* American Indian Law Review 16(2):319–75.

Hanson, Stephen Cosby

1980 United States v Sioux Nation: Political Questions, Moral Imperative, and the National Honor. American Indian Law Review 8:459–84.

Harring, Sidney L.

1994 Crow Dog's Case. Cambridge: Cambridge University Press.

Hasselstrom, Linda

1991 Land Circle: Writings Collected from the Land. Golden, Colo.: Fulcrum Press.

Holt, H. Barry, and Gary Forrester

1990 Digest of American Indian Law: Cases and Chronology. Littleton, Colo.: F. B. Rothman.

Hoxie, Frederick E.

1984 A Final Promise: The Campaign to Assimilate the Indians, 1880–1920. Lincoln: University of Nebraska Press.

Institute for the Development of Indian Law

1974 Treaties and Agreements and the Proceedings of the Treaties and Agreements of the Tribes and Bands of the Sioux Nation. Washington, D.C.: Institute for the Development of Indian Law.

Jacobs, Emma, ed.

1996 [1983] Dimming Trails, Fading Memories: Recollections of Mortimer and Julia Clifford. Unpublished manuscript in author's possession.

1985 Dimming Trails, Fading Memories: Recollections of Art and Mary Rolf. Unpublished manuscript in author's possession.

Jorgensen, Joseph G.

1984 Land is Cultural, So Is Commodity: The Locus of Differences among Indians, Cowboys, Sod-Busters, and Environmentalists. Journal of Ethnic Studies 12(3):1–21.

Kappler, Charles J.

1904 Indian Affairs: Laws and Treaties. Volume 2 (Treaties). Washington: Government Printing Office.

Kurkiala, Mikael

1997 Building the Nation Back Up: The Politics of Identity on the Pine Ridge Indian Reservation. Stockholm, Sweden: Acta Universitatis Press.

LaFave, LeAnn Larson

1984 South Dakota's Forced Fee Indian Land Claims: Will Landowners Be Liable for Government's Wrongdoing? South Dakota Law Review 30:59–102.

Laslett, Peter (ed.)

1963 John Locke: Two Treatises of Government. New York: The New English Library Limited.

Lazarus, Edward

1991 Black Hills, White Justice. New York: Harper Collins Publishers.

Lewis, Emily H., ed.

1980 Wo'wakita, Reservation Recollections: A People's History of the Allen Issue Station District on the Pine Ridge Indian Reservation of South Dakota. Sioux Falls, S. Dak.: Center for Western Studies, Augustana College.

Long, Mamie B.

1975 A Pioneer Story. Unpublished manuscript.

Lyman, Stanley D.

1991 Wounded Knee 1973: A Personal Account. Lincoln: University of Nebraska Press.

Macgregor, Gordon

1946 Warriors Without Weapons: A Study of the Society and Personality Development of the Pine Ridge Sioux. Chicago: University of Chicago Press.

Martindale, Don, and R. Galen Hanson

1971 [1969] Small Town and the Nation: The Conflict of Local and Translocal Forces. Westport, Conn.: Greenwood.

Matthews, Anne

1992 Where the Buffalo Roam: The Storm over the Revolutionary Plan to Restore America's Great Plains. New York: Grove Press.

Matthiessen, Peter

1991 [1980] In the Spirit of Crazy Horse. New York: Penguin Press.

McDonnell, Janet A.

> 1991 The Dispossession of the American Indian, 1887–1934. Bloomington: Indiana University Press.
>
> 1989 Competency Commissions and Indian Land Policy, 1913–1920. South Dakota History 11:21–34.

Means, Russell, with Marvin J. Wolf

> 1995 Where White Men Fear to Tread: The Autobiography of Russell Means. New York: St. Martin's Press.

Mekeel, Scudder

> 1932 Discussion of Culture Change as Illustrated by Material from a Teton-Dakota Community. American Anthropologist. 34:274–85.
>
> 1936 The Economy of a Modern Teton Dakota Community. Yale University Publications in Anthropology 6.

Moore, Sally Falk

> 1986 Social Facts and Fabrications. Cambridge: Cambridge University Press.

Myerhoff, Barbara, and Stephen Mongulla

> 1986 The Los Angeles Jews' "Walk for Solidarity": Parade, Festival, Pilgrimage. In Symbolizing America, edited by Hervé Varenne, 119–35. Lincoln: University of Nebraska Press.

Nagel, Joane

> 1997 American Indian Ethnic Renewal: Red Power and the Resurgence of Identity and Culture. New York: Oxford University Press.

Nelson, Paula M.

> 1986 After the West Was Won: Homesteaders and Town-Builders in Western South Dakota, 1900–1917. Iowa City: University of Iowa Press.

One Feather, Vivian

> 1974 Tiyošpayes. Pine Ridge, S. Dak.: Oglala Sioux Culture Center, Red Cloud Indian School.

Otis, D. S.

> 1973 [1934] The Dawes Act and the Allotment of Indian Land. Norman: University of Oklahoma Press.

Popper, Frank J.

> 1984 The Ambiguous End of the Sagebrush Rebellion. In Land Reform, American Style, edited by Charles C. Geisler and Frank J. Popper, 117–28. Totowa, N.J.: Rowman and Allanheld.

Powers, Marla N.

> 1986 Oglala Women: Myth, Ritual, and Reality. Chicago: University of Chicago Press.

Powers, William K.

> 1977 Oglala Religion. Lincoln: University of Nebraska Press.

Prucha, Francis Paul

    1984 The Great Father: The United States Government and the American Indians. 2 vols. Lincoln: University of Nebraska Press.

Prucha, Francis Paul, ed.

    1990 Documents of United States Indian Policy. 2d ed., expanded. Lincoln: University of Nebraska Press.

Robertson, Paul M.

    1995 The Power of the Land: Identity, Ethnicity, and Class among the Oglala Lakota. Ph.D. diss., Graduate School of the Union Institute.

Rood, David S., and Allan R. Taylor

    1996 Sketch of Lakhota, a Siouan Language. *In* Handbook of North American Indians, vol. 17, Language, edited by Ives Goddard, 440–82. Washington: Smithsonian Institution.

Royce, Anya Peterson

    1982 Ethnic Identity: Strategies of Diversity. Bloomington: Indiana University Press.

Schneider, David M.

    1980 American Kinship: A Cultural Account. Chicago: University of Chicago Press.

Schusky, Ernest L.

    1986 The Evolution of Indian Leadership on the Great Plains, 1750–1950. American Indian Quarterly 10:65–82.

Smith, Henry Nash

    1978 Virgin Land: The American West as Symbol and Myth. Cambridge, Mass.: Harvard University Press.

Spicer, Edward H.

    1971 Persistent Cultural Systems. Science 40(2) 795–800.

    1994 The Nations of a State. *In* American Indian Persistence and Resurgence, edited by Karl Kroeber, 27–49. Durham: Duke University Press.

Tiller, Veronica E. Vilarde

    1996 American Indian Reservations and Trust Areas Economic Development Administration. Washington D.C.: U.S. Department of Commerce.

Turner, Victor

    1967 The Forest of Symbols: Aspects of Ndembu Ritual. Ithaca, N.Y.: Cornell University Press.

Utley, Robert M.

    1963 The Last Days of the Sioux Nation. New Haven: Yale University Press.

U.S. Government

    1936 The Future of the Great Plains: Report of the Great Plains Committee. Washington, D.C.: U.S. Government Printing Office.

Wagoner, Paula L.

    1994 Ambivalent Identities: Processes of Marginalization and Exclusion. MacArthur Scholar Series, Occasional Paper 25. Bloomington: Indiana University Press.

    1997a Ambivalent Identities: Land, Blood, and U.S. Federal Policy in Bennett County, South Dakota. Ph.D. diss., Indiana University.

    1997b Surveying Justice: The Problematics of Overlapping Jurisdictional Domains in Indian Country. Droit et cultures 33(1) 21–52.

    1998a Coming Home to What?: The Poetics of Non-Meaning in Martin, South Dakota. *In* Interpreting Cultures: A Symposium, edited by Paula L. Wagoner and Mindy J. Morgan, 1–7. Bloomington: Indiana University Department of Anthropology.

    1998b An Unsettled Frontier: Land, Blood, and U.S. Federal Policy, *In* Property Relations, edited by C. M. Hann, 124–41. London: Cambridge University Press.

Walker, James R.

    1980 Lakota Belief and Ritual. Lincoln: University of Nebraska Press.

    1982 Lakota Society. Lincoln: University of Nebraska Press.

Wallace, Anthony F. C., and Raymond D. Fogelson

    1965 The Identity struggle. *In* Intensive Family Therapy: Theoretical and Practical Aspects, edited by Ivan Boszomenyi-Nagi and James L. Framo, 365–406. New York: Harper and Row.

Washburn, Wilcomb

    1971 Red Man's Land / White Man's Law: A Study of the Past and Present Status of the American Indian. New York: Charles Scribner's and Sons.

Wax, Murray L., Rosalie H. Wax, Robert V. Dumant, Jr., and Gerald One Feather

    1964 Formal Education in an American Indian Community. Social Problems 11(4), supplement 1–125.

Wax, Murray L., Rosalie H. Wax, and Robert V. Dumant, Jr., with the assistance of Roselyn Holyrock and Gerald One Feather.

    1989 Formal Education in an American Indian Community. Atlanta: Emory University.

Wax, Rosalie

    1971 Doing Fieldwork: Warnings and Advice. Chicago: University of Chicago Press.

Webb, Walter Prescott

    1931 The Great Plains. Boston: Ginn and Company.

White, Richard

    1991 "It's Your Misfortune and None of My Own": A New History of the American West. Norman: University of Oklahoma Press.

Williams, Robert A., Jr.

      1990 The American Indian in Western Legal Thought: The Discourses of Conquest. New York: Oxford University Press.

ARCHIVAL MATERIALS

Pierre, S. Dak., South Dakota State Historical Resource Center

  Brennan Family Papers (H72.2)

  Council proceedings, April 1, 1909.

  Council minutes, April 15, 1909.

  Letterbook 1906–1909.

Washington, D.C., U.S. National Archives

Superintendent's Annual Narrative and Statistical Report. August, 1910. Microfilm Publication M1011, Roll 106.

Indian Census Rolls, Pine Ridge Reservation, 1885–1943. Microfilm Publication M595.

NEWSPAPERS

Bennett County Booster I. Martin, South Dakota.

Bennett County Booster II. Martin, South Dakota.

Indian Country Today

INDEX

mixedbloods (*continued*)
   as cultural interpreters and brokers, 13, 61;
   economic advantages of, 61, 137 n.4; and
   education, 62, 128; fullbloods viewed by, 58–
   59, 60, 62–63, 137 n.3; and identity, 47, 91;
   kinship expectations violated by, 13; Lakota
   word for, 61; and the land, 60, 75, 126; and
   the opening of Bennett County, 43; political
   role of, 41, 42, 61, 75, 126; situational ethnicity of, 128; viewed as marginal, 13, 61, 75;
   viewed by fullbloods, 13, 42, 44, 60, 61–62,
   75, 126, 127; viewed by non-Indians, 1, 61,
   62, 126, 127; viewed by whites, 13, 44, 60, 75;
   worldview of, 51
Myerhoff, Barbara, and Stephen Mongulla, 48

Native Americans. *See* fullbloods; Indians;
   Lakotas
"neighboring," 7, 59, 78
non-Indians: and Euro-American culture, 127;
   and forced relocation, 115–16, 128, 139 n.20;
   fullbloods viewed by, 59, 60, 64; homesteading, 40–44, 136 n.9; and identity, 47, 92; and
   Lakota wakes, 86; mixedbloods viewed by,
   61, 62, 126, 127; race viewed by oldtimers
   among, 102; Wounded Knee viewed by, 79.
   See also whites
North Dakota, 135 n.1

Of Civil Government (Locke), 70–71
Oglala Lakotas. *See* Lakotas
Oglala Sioux Tribal Council, 64
Oglala Sioux Tribe, 53, 85
outsiders, 18; author as, 29; distrust of, 7–9,
   125; and the homecoming bonfire, 29, 30;
   impact of, 32; marrying into non-Indian
   families, 51–52; and regional identity, 93

Peltier, Leonard, 23
Pine Ridge Indian Reservation: and Bennett County, 3, 18, 39, 44, 98, 108, 113, 136
   n.3, 139 n.14; diminishment of, 113; ethnographic inquiries, 12; and Fall River County,
   138 n.3; political role of mixedbloods on,
   41; residents from, at homecoming, 30;
   sports rivalry with Bennett County, 20; and
   Wounded Knee, 93

Plenty Bear, 42, 43
pluralism, 124
Popper, Frank, and Deborah, 8
Powers, Marla N., 12
Powers, William K., 12
Prucha, Francis Paul, 39, 74
Public Law 280, 139 n.11

Quick, Herbert, 3

race, 7–8; arbitrariness of, 13–14; and class,
   13; and crime, 110, 111, 114, 123–24; and law
   enforcement, 104, 108; recalled by oldtimers,
   102; and taxes, 57
race relations, 130; and checkerboard jurisdiction, 103, 115, 116, 139 n.19; and economic
   crisis, 115; and the Indian Reorganization
   Act, 102, 103
racism, 23, 75–76, 88, 114, 124
ranchers, 2, 5, 6, 14; and federal programs, 52,
   135 n.4
Rand McNally and Company, 2, 135 n.1
rations, 99, 138 n.6
Red Cloud, 58
Red Cloud Agency, 98
reservations, 34, 35, 98–99; alcohol on, 111;
   jurisdiction on, 96–97, 138 n.3; and non-
   Indians, 101–2; rations on, 99, 138 n.6
ritual: defined, 15; and symbol, 15–16
Robertson, Paul, 12
Roosevelt, Theodore, 35
Rosebud Reservation, 20, 39, 41, 42, 113
Rosebud Sioux Tribe, 138 n.2
Royce, Anya Peterson, 50

Santa Clara Pueblo v Martinez, 114, 139 n.18
Santee Dakotas, 63
Schneider, David, 67–68
Schusky, Ernest, 61
Sells, Cato, 73, 74
shooting, 18, 78–79, 93, 117; arraignment, 82–
   85; first night wake, 81–82; and Means, 87,
   89–90; newspaper articles on, 86–87, 124;
   and non-Indians, 124; and outsiders, 87, 124;
   preliminary trial, 87–90; and race, 123–24;
   and rumors of retribution, 81; second night
   wake, 80, 85–87; vigil for victim of, 79–81

Short Grass, 64
Sioux Nation, 34, 36, 138 n.6
social fields, 11, 12, 18, 20, 32, 46–48, 51, 52, 57, 61, 75, 91, 92, 94, 104, 115, 116, 123
South Dakota, 2–3, 34, 52, 135 n.1
sovereignty, 50, 114
Speaking of Indians (Deloria), 65–66
Spicer, Edward, 46–47
Steele, John Yellowbird, 122
Sword, George, 66
symbols, 15–16, 123, 126

Teller, Henry M., 35
thiyóšpaye, 44; defined, 7, 67
Treaty of 1868, 34, 36, 60, 98
Turner, Ted, 134
Turner, Victor, 15
Turning Hawk, Charles, 42
Tuthill SD, 78

veterans, 119–20

Walker, James R., 12
Wallace, Anthony F. C., 91

Wall Drug, 2–3
Warrior symbol, 125; appropriate at adoption of, 48–49, 50; Lakota grievances concerning, 20, 21, 22–23, 28, 29
Wax, Murray, et al., 12
Wax, Rosalie, 12
West River, 52
Wheeler-Howard Act, 137 n.2
Where White Men Fear to Tread (Means), 137 n.8
White, Richard, 38
whites, 17, 63–64; attitudes toward, 12–13; as cultural rather than racial category, 44; full-bloods viewed by, 58–59, 137 n.3; hierarchy among, 137 n.5; interactions with fullbloods, 64; mixedbloods viewed by, 13, 44, 60, 75; worldview of, 51. *See also* non-Indians
Wild Horse Butte Powwow, 117–21, 124, 131
Wilson, Dick, 109
Wounded Knee, 109, 133; and Bennett County, 79; takeover by AIM, 76, 87, 89, 93

Yankton Reservation, 39
Yellow Thunder, Raymond, 87, 89